MW01274590

# THOUGHTS
# from
# REFLECTIONS

Finally, brethren, whatsoever things are
true, whatsoever things *are* honest,
whatsoever things *are* just, whatsoever
things *are* pure, whatsoever things *are*
lovely, whatsoever things *are* of good
report; if *there be* any virtue, and if *there
be* any praise, think on these things
Philippians 4:9 NKJV

BY

# REV. RUDY YOST

### Cartoons by
### Dr. Joe McKeever

PUBLISHED BY YOSTCRAFT
Printed by CreateSpace

THOUGHTS from REFLECTIONS

Printer in the United States of America


October 2016


"

# INTRODUCTION

I walked into my office, and my secretary had a big grin on her face. "Your books have arrived!" she said.

I opened the box and took out one of the books which had the title, **THOUGHTS from REFLECTIONS.**
"I have to call Bob and Wilma and tell them that I have a surprise for them," I said.

(Bob and Wilma were a fictitious couple that I created in my last book. In the book I pictured having a Bible study with them in my office. The chapters in the book served as individual sessions when we met together. They represented all those people that I have ministered to when I was a pastor. I have received many comments that it made the book personal to the reader as they read the book. . I have continued to use them in this book.).

I went into my office and picked up the phone and Bob answered. "I have a great surprise for you and Wilma. If Wilma will bake an apple pie, my wife and I will come over and tell you what it is and show it to you."

Wilma was in the room, and Bob explained to her that the pastor had a big surprise to show them if she would bake an apple pie for him.

She said, "You bet, Pastor." She was noted for her great apple pies. "Tell the Pastor that I will get busy baking that pie, and he and his wife can come over at 7:30 tonight to enjoy it with a big scoop of vanilla ice cream on it." "

Wilma went on to ask Bob if the pastor had said what the surprise was.

"We will have to wait," said Bob.

"Okay, Pastor, we will see you tonight," Bob said as he hung up his phone.

My wife and I arrived at 7:30 and were greeted by Wilma who was anxious to find out what the surprise was.

As we entered their home I gave each of them a wrapped present. Wilma quickly tore the present open and gave out a squeal as she saw the cover of the book that was in her hand. "You have written a new book! "she exclaimed as she noted the title, **THOUGHTS from REFLECTIONS.**

"I have been working on the book without you knowing about it, and here it is! I hope you will enjoy it. Read the preface and it will tell all about the book," I shared as we sat down.

.We spent the rest of the evening enjoying the pie and discussing the book and what I had included in it.

As we were getting ready to leave, Bob said, "Let me offer a prayer to the Lord that He will use the book to put holy clean thoughts in the reader's minds, which is based on the Bible verse on the front cover of. "**THOUGHTS from REFLECTIONS.**

Bob closed our time together in prayer.

You the readers are my Bob and Wilma. God bless you as you read the book.

# ..... . CONTENTS

### CLIPPINGS & ILLUSTRATIONS

# DEDICATION

To God the Father who has planned my life and made  me
a member of His family,

To God the Son, the Lord Jesus Christ, who created me,
saved me, and prays for me, and

To the blessed Holy Spirit, who dwells in me, prays for me,
and guides me in my daily life.

Secondly, I dedicate this book to my wife, Barbara,
whom God chose to be my wife for these 57 years and has
been a tremendous blessing in my life.

# BIBLE TRANSLATIONS QUOTED

Quotations from the Bible will be taken from several translations. The icon for a translation will follow the translation source except those verses quoted from the Authorized King James Version which will be the basic translation used.

The AUTHORIZED KING JAM ES VERSION,The Oxford University Press, New York, INC. 1909, 1917, Copyright renewed, 1937,1945.

# PREFACE

## WHAT DO YOU THINK ABOUT?

In these times we are exposed to all kinds of thoughts we get from what we read, hear, and view. Our minds are like a computer and whatever we put in them are there until we die. I know there are things I wish I had not put into my mind that have come up when I didn't expect them to and wished I had never allowed them to enter.

God spoke through the Apostle Paul in the Bible that the believer needs to carefully consider what he or she thinks about.

*Finally, brethren, whatever things are true, whatever things are noble, whatever things are just, whatever things are pure, whatever things are lovely, whatever things are of good report, if there is any virtue and if there is anything praiseworthy—meditate on these things.* Philippians 4:8 NKJV

**It is my goal in this book to fill your mind with thoughts that will help achieve *those goals to think about* in your thought life.**

There are many ways a pastor ministers to his congregation and one of the ways is through the printed page. During my teenage years I would listen to Rev. Al Salter on the radio every Sunday morning before I went to church. He published a four page publication entitled *STRENGTH* which contained poems, a short challenge to the reader, and stories about living. It really met my need as a teenager. I also listened to THE HAVEN OF REST broadcast during the week, and they sent out a publication, *The Log of the Good Ship Grace,* that also featured special articles, poems, and sometimes a short devotion by Shipmate Bob, the founder.

Dr. M.R.DeHaan also ministered with a detailed Bible study titled THE RADIO BIBLE CLASS that was heard on Sunday morning. He sent out booklets containing his radio messages.

I clipped the poems, stories and messages from all those publications figuring I might use them some day when I became a pastor.

When I became a pastor, I went about creating a little publication for each church I served containing positive thoughts which were patterned after the publications I had saved.

In 2002 I made the decision to create a publication that I would send on a nonprofit basis to those who wanted to receive it titled REFLECTIONS. The demand for it grew to where it was received all the way to the east coast and several missionaries in other parts of the world.

I stopped publishing **REFLECTIONS** in 2013 and wrote a book titled **REFLECTIONS OF A PASTOR.** I wanted to share what it is like behind the scenes being a pastor, sharing some of my experiences, and what I have learned from them.

My second book was entitled **ETERNALLY SECURE IN GOD'S FAMILY** which dealt with the question: Can I be cast out of the family of God after I have become a believer and a member of God's family? It was published in 2014.

This book, **THOUGHTS from REFLECTIONS,** brings together some of my favorite articles that I wrote in REFLECTIONS, as well as some of my favorite clipping and articles written by others that I have gathered through the years. Some of them are about what is involved in a

Christian's life such as encouragement, challenges, instruction, personal experiences,(Little Lost Dog), and most of all God's love, provision, and His plan for the future which are based on Scripture. Below each article I have written is the year I wrote it.

In some instances I have listed a passage of Scripture related to the article that the reader could use as a meditation for the day entitled Bible verses.

I want to thank Dr. Joe McKeever for the use of his cartoons that have made me laugh, touched my heart ,and made me think as a pastor. Joe is a retired Baptist pastor who is still active in the ministry. He furnished the Baptist Press with cartoons through the years and has an active website on Facebook.

The scenic pictures have been taken by my son Paul and grandson, Jared.Yost.

God bless you as you read this book and think about what has been written.

# LITTLE LOST DOG
July 1991

The other day when I was taking some mail to the post office, an incident happened that again reminded me that God really cares.

As I was driving down Willamette Blvd. I saw a white wirehaired dog that was trying to cross the street. He ran in front of my car and I braked and a line of cars behind me braked too. (I was sure glad they did.). An oncoming car braked too for the little dog.

I parked my car and went into the post office and on returning to the church, I saw the dog again which had distance two blocks away. He was running hard because he had seen two kids with a big black dog on the street corner. I ran down the street trying to keep tract of the dog because I feared he would be hit by car because he was so mixed up and was going into the busy streets in St. Johns. I lost sight of him again. I went back to my car and drove into the St. John's area hoping to find him and hoped to catch him to give him some help, but I couldn't find him.

I decided to return to the church, but as I drove back I prayed that God would take care of that little white dog which was lost.

All of a sudden I caught sight of him as I was driving back to the church and pulled up next to him. He looked up at me, but kept running. He really had fear in his eyes. I went up the street following him in my car.

A lady in a black car met me at an intersection, rolled down her window and asked if it was my dog.

I said no to her and said it was a little lost dog.
She said: "He's going to be hit by a car."

I replied, "I know."

We both pursued the little dog, but whenever we got near him he would run away faster. I finally lost sight of him because he turned a corner after I had gone past it.

I again said a special prayer for that little white dog. He had no collar and looked dirty like he had been travelling a long distance. I had a lump in my throat because I wanted to help him, but he wouldn't let me. All I could do was to pray for him.

There are two lessons in this experience.

First of all, God cares about little lost dogs and I knew I could pray for him and God would hear my prayer. The Lord Jesus said, "Are not two sparrows sold for a farthing? and one of them shall not fall on the ground without your Father.". ( Matthew 10:29), and God knew all about that little; dog and would take care of him.

Secondly, it reminded me of an individual who is scared about life and the future, but rejects God reaching out His hand to him or her to find a place of refuge and safety. I would have loved to take that little dog in my arms and say "you're safe now and I will help you."

God has a wonderful plan for a person if he or she will stop and let Him take care of them when they invite Jesus Christ into their life.

Maybe you're one of those individuals who is scared about life .Why not stop and invite Jesus Christ to come into your life. He has been following you. Why not stop and let Him come and take care of you. *For God so loved the world that He gave His his only Son that whoever* (that is you) *believes in Him shall not perish but have everlasting.life.*(John 3:16)

# A PENNY REMINDER

September 2003

This month I want to share something I read that I haven't been able to get out of my mind. I came across it just this last month again. I hope you will enjoy reading it [Several years ago, a friend of mine and her husband were invited to spend the weekend at the husband's employer's home. My friend, Arlene, was nervous about the weekend. The boss was very wealthy, with a fine home on the waterway, and cars costing more than her house.

The first day and evening went well, and Arlene was delighted to have this rare glimpse into how the very wealthy live. The husband's employer was quite generous as a host, and took them to the finest restaurants. Arlene knew she would never have the opportunity to indulge in this kind of extravagance again, so was enjoying herself immensely.

As the three of them were about to enter an exclusive restaurant that evening, the boss was walking slightly ahead of Arlene and her husband. He stopped suddenly, looking down on the pavement for a long, silent moment. Arlene wondered if she was supposed to pass him. There was a penny on the ground and he picked it up.

He held it up and smiled, then put it in his pocket as if he had found a great treasure. How absurd! What need did this man have for a single penny? Why would he even take the time to stop and pick it up?

Throughout dinner, the entire scene nagged at her. Finally, she could stand it no longer. She casually mentioned that her daughter had a coin collection, and asked if the penny he had found had been of some value.

15

A smile crept across the man's face as he reached into his pocket for the penny and held it out for her to see. She had seen many pennies before! What was the point of this?

"Look at it." He said. "Read what it says."

She read the words "United States of America."

"No, not that; read further."

"One cent?"

"No, keep reading."

"In God we Trust."

"Yes!"

"And?"

"And if I trust in God, the name of God is holy, even on a coin. Whenever I find a coin I see that inscription. It is written on every single United States coin, but we never seem to notice it! God drops a message right in front of me telling me to trust Him? Who am I to pass it by? When I see a coin, I pray. I stop to see if my trust IS in God at that moment. I pick the coin up as a response to God; that I do trust in Him. For a short time, at least, I cherish it as if it were gold. I think it is God's way of starting a conversation with me. Lucky for me, God is patient and pennies are plentiful!"

When I was out shopping today, I found a penny on the sidewalk. I stopped and picked it up, and realized that I had to laugh. Yes, God, I get the message.

It seems that I have been finding an inordinate number of pennies in the last three months, but then, pennies are plentiful. And God is patient.]   Author Unknown,   Christian Clippings

BIBLE VERSE: PROVERBS 3:5,6.

## COMPATIBLE CHRISTIANS
November 2003

Recently our TV set bit the dust and died, so we purchased a new one. As I began to set-up the TV set, I went about trying to code the VCR remote with the new TV. It wasn't compatible even thought I fed several codes into the remote. I ended up going to Radio Shack and purchasing a Universal Remote that was compatible with both the TV and the VCR.

As I thought about my experience, I thought about the attitude of some Christians toward other Christians. Some Christians feel that their denomination is the only one that has all the truth, and like the remote, aren't very compatible because others don't believe like they do.

The church in the town of Corinth, where the Apostle Paul ministered, faced a problem of unity. He wrote: "I appeal to you, brothers, in the name of our Lord Jesus Christ, that all of you agree with one another so that there may be no divisions among you, and that you may be perfectly united in mind and thought. My brothers, some from Chloe's household have informed me that there are quarrels among you. What I mean is this: One of you says, "I follow Paul"; another, "I follow Apollos" another, "I follow Cephas"; still another, "I follow Christ". Is Christ divided? Was Paul crucified for you?" (1 Corinthians 1:10-13 NIV)

Other Christians have problems getting along with other people who are in their own church.

In Jesus' day, the disciples of Jesus had the same problem. We read in Luke 9:49, 50 John the disciple saying: "Master," "we saw a man driving out demons in your name and we tried to stop him, because he is not one

17

of us." Jesus answered: "Do not stop him,... for whoever is not against you is for you." NIV

Paul, in writing to those in the church at Galatia, wrote: "The entire law is summed up in a single command: "Love your neighbor as yourself." If you keep on biting and devouring each other, watch out or you will be destroyed by each other." ( Galatians 5:14, 15 NIV)

In his book, Great Church Fights, Leslie B. Flynn tells how two porcupines in the freezing north country of Canada huddled together to keep warm. But because they were pricked by each other's quills, they moved apart. Soon they were shivering again and had to lie side by side once more for their own survival. They needed each other.

As Christians we need each other.

H.G.Boggs wrote the following article in Our Daily Bread entitled "UNITED BRETHREN"

ALMOST 25 years ago at Winona Lake, Indiana, I had the privilege of meeting the renowned song leader Homer Rodeheaver. During a visit in his home at "Rainbow Point," he related many incidents from his expansive career and then told this humorous but pointed story:

" A gentleman who belonged to a Plymouth Brethren assembly met with a serious accident in which his leg was crushed while working in an iron mine at Duluth, Minnesota. He was rushed to a Catholic hospital where it became necessary to amputate his badly injured limb. An Episcopal surgeon performed the operation, and he was cared for by a Presbyterian nurse. He subsequently advertised for a wooden leg in a Congregational paper. A Methodist widow, whose crippled husband had been a Baptist, took out of storage his artificial leg and sent it by a Lutheran messenger to this needy Christian. When the amputee learned the full story he said, "I guess I'm now

**"united brethren"!** We smile and yet we recognize a basic truth underlying that incident . There is a fundamental tie between Christians which the various denominational differences cannot sever. This spiritual unity—akin to that which exists between the Lord Jesus and His Heavenly Father –is there by virtue of Christ's redeeming blood. All true believers are actually one in the blessed "mystical body" called the Church (Eph. 1::22, 23; 2:16, 20-22; 4:15, 16). Although we who are Christians regret the friction that often arises due to denominational bias, in a greater sense, we are "united brethren"! Our Daily Bread

Billy Graham and his son, Franklin Graham, have been such an example of unity in Christ when their origination holds a crusade. The gospel is never compromised, and the denominations work together to win people to Jesus Christ.

We need to ask ourselves a question—are we compatible with other Christians in the unity of the Holy Spirit? (Ephesians 4:1-6).

# The Whale Said "Thank You"

(This story was featured in *Christian Clippings*)

"If you read a recent front page story of the *San Francisco Chronicle,* you would have read about a female humpback whale that had become entangled in a spider web of crab traps and lines. She was weighed down by hundreds of pounds of traps that caused her to struggle to stay afloat. She also had hundreds of yards of line rope wrapped around her body, her tail, her torso, a line tugging in her mouth. A fisherman spotted her just east of the Farallon Islands (outside the Golden Gate and radioed an environmental group for help. Within a few hours, the rescue team arrived and determined that she was so bad off, the only way to save her was to dive in and untangle her.

They worked for hours with curved knives and eventually freed her. When she was free, the divers say she swam in what seemed like joyous circles. She then came back to each and every diver, one at a time, nudged them, and pushed them gently around: she was thanking them. Some said it was the most incredibly beautiful experience of their lives. The guy who cut the rope out of her mouth said her eyes were following him the whole time, and he will never be the same.

May you love, be so blessed and fortunate to be surrounded by people who will help you get untangled from the things that are binding you. And may you always know the joy of giving and receiving gratitude."

Christian Clippings, Oct-Nov 2009

# HONORING GOD'S NAMES
August 2003

When we invite Jesus Christ into our life we become a member of God's family. We have access to our Heavenly Father in heaven through prayer.

Peter states in 1 Peter 2:9 that we are members of a royal priesthood again, signifying that we now have a special relationship with the Father.

The writer of Hebrews gives encouragement. [6]Let us therefore come boldly unto the throne of grace, that we may obtain mercy, and find grace to help in time of need." (Hebrews 4:16). It is because Jesus Christ is our high priest under whom we serve as priests. (Hebrews 4:14-16.)

Then we come to the example that Jesus gave His disciples how to pray. They had asked Him to teach them to pray and lovingly He gave a model prayer with guidelines for prayer. (Matthew 6:9-13) This month I want to focus on the phrase. in the prayer *"Our Father in heaven, hallowed be your name."* The word hallowed means: "to set apart" with the idea to respect Hisholy name and hold it dear to our heart.

Something I have done recently is to take a name of God and concentrate on it for a week in my prayers. It has been such a blessing to open my prayer time with the Lord concentrating on one of His names and use it for a time of praise to Him. I have done research in the Scriptures and have found where that name is introduced and revealed by God. This helps me when I talk to Him about His name.

Let me give some examples of some of the names of God that one can use.

*"Jehovah"* The name in the Hebrew means "self-existent" "to be" "to become" Jesus claimed this name in John 8:58 and they tried to stone Him because of it. It appears in the Old Testament in capital letters **LORD.**

Jehovah appears first in Genesis 2:7 in creation and in Genesis 3:9-13 when He sought Adam and Eve.

He revealed this name to Moses from the burning Bush in Exodus 3:14, 15. This name is used to give comfort to those who are weak in Isaiah 40:28-31. This name appears throughout the Old Testament, but these are a few instances of its appearance.

Applying this name to our prayer time in praise we can praise Him for His creation, for revealing Himself to Moses and making His plan for redeeming Israel, for giving us strength each day to live our life through His indwelling power of the Holy Spirit.

In the Old Testament *Jehovah* is connected with another name which makes it a compound name. One could take a week for each compound name as I did recently. Examples of these are: **Jehovah Elohim** =Creator , Redeemer of Man Genesis 2:7-1; **Jehovah-Jirah**="the LORD will provide "Jesus 22:13, 14, **Jehovah-rapha**= "the LORD who heals you" Exodus 15:26; **Jehovah-nissi**= "the LORD is my banner" Exodus 27:8-15, **Jehovah-shalom**= "the LORD is peace" or "the LORD send peace, (Judges 6 Jeremiah 23:6 [the name that relates to the prophecy of Israel's conversion and restoration]), **Jehovah-shammah**= "the LORD is there" Ezekiel 48:35 which speaks of His abiding presence.)

During the week we might take each day to praise Jesus because He said He was the great **"I AM"**.

*"56Your father Abraham rejoiced to see my day: and he saw it, and was glad. 57Then said the Jews unto him, Thou art not yet fifty years old, and hast thou seen*

*Abraham? [58]Jesus said unto them, Verily, verily, I say unto you, Before Abraham was, I am."* (John 8:56-58 — The Good Shepherd, The Door, The Bread of Life, The Bright and Morning Star, Alpha and Omega, The Beginning and the End, The Light of the World, The Resurrection and The Life, Your Master and Lord, The True Vine, The Way, The Truth, The Life.

Yes, God has some personal names His family call Him by. I challenge you to try addressing Him by a different name when you pray.

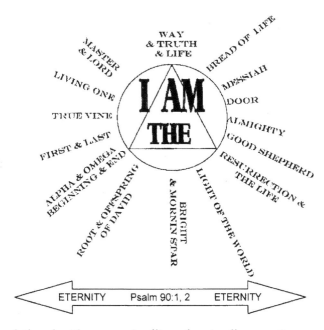

Lord, thou hast been our dwelling place in all generations. Before the mountains were brought forth, or ever thou hadst formed the earth and the world, even from everlasting to everlasting, thou *art* God.

Illustration 1

# DEDICATION

Lord, make me a channel of Thy peace:
That where there is hatred—
    I may bring love,
That where there is wrong—
    I may bring the spirit of forgiveness,
That where there is discord--
    I may bring harmony,
That where there is error—
    I may bring truth
That where there is doubt—
    I may bring faith,
That where there is despair—
    That I may bring hope,
That where there are shadows—
    I may bring light,
That where there is sadness—
    I may bring joy,
Lord, grant that I may seek rather
    to comfort—than to be comforted,
To understand—than to be understood;
To love—than to be loved;
For
    It is by giving—that one receives;
    It is by self-forgetting—that one finds;
    It is by forgetting—that one is forgiven;
    It is by dying—that one awakens
        to eternal life.
                  -Francis of Assisi

# "MY ICE-CREAM CONE DIARY"
May 2004

•

Recently I have been having fun rereading the books in a series entitled *he Sugar Creek Gang*. They are books that were especially for children. My mother would read a chapter each night to my brother and me when we were young.. He always left us hanging on a limb at the end of each chapter. My mother said she would go and read on in the book after she left us to go to sleep because she wondered what would happen too.

Paul Hutchens was an evangelist during the early years of his life. He reached thousands of folk with the gospel but he came down with TB and it was a real blow in his life. He wondered why God allowed this to happen in his life when he was having such a fruitful ministry.

In his biography he writes of an incident in his life as a preschool boy. His parents were poor and to have some money in his pocket was something special. He and his folks lived on a farm. His parents took him to a county fair in Lebanon, Indiana. He found himself alone by an ice-cream stand amidst the sounds of the merry-go round and the barkers in their booths.

He writes,:" Waiting near an ice-cream stand, noticed curiously that people and people and more people came to stand, tossed money down, accepted ice-cream cones, picked up change, and went happily away. PH with not one penny in pocket or hand...People continued to come. Ice cream looked so good, so cool, so sweet so satisfying to hungry boy. Different colors—pink, white, chocolate. Would like to have ice-cream cone. Thinks, and re-thinks. Others lay down money receive cones, got money in exchange move on, munching cones .Mouth waters for cold ice-cream cone...Hot day...Others get not only cones but get their money back as well,--some of them much more money it seems, than had been laid down in the place".

Well, Paul Hutchens, the little boy, appeared before the ice-cream man who was smiling and calling out "Ice cream...Ice cream" and the ice-cream man gives him a cone and PH waits for the change.

He waited for a second, felt foolish and goes into the crowd. He then hears the man shouting "Hey Kid, where's your nickel?" He ran back, gave the man the ice-cream cone and then says, "Here take it" and runs back into the crowd, ashamed and confused."

Paul Hutchens wrote that he called this experience his "Ice Cream Cone Diary." He said in his autobiography that he had had experiences that he could list in his *Ice Cream Cone Diary* noting that there were times in his life when he thought something was going to happen, but the Lord had different plans for him. He couldn't understand why God had taken him out of the ministry of evangelism and put him flat on his back in bed. But God had other plans for his life and led him to start writing. He wrote several novels including the *Sugar Creek Gang* books that resulted in him reaching far more people and children than he ever imagined. Those books are still reaching individuals today with the gospel message included in them as well as challenges to live a godly life.

I know I have experienced "Ice Cream Cone Diary" experiences in my life. But I have found through each experience God has led in my life to accomplish something that I never dreamed would take place. There is a poem I have included in *Reflections* in the past entitled *Things Just Don't Happen* that appears again on the next page that helps put this into words. There are several Scriptures that also share how God works in this way.

Jeremiah 29:11 .[11]For I know the thoughts that I think toward you, saith the LORD, thoughts of peace, and not of evil, to give you an expected end."

Isaiah 55:8, 9 [8]For my thoughts *are* not your thoughts, neither *are* your ways my ways, saith the LORD. [9]For *as* the heavens are higher than the earth, so are my ways higher than your ways, and my thoughts than your thoughts

We can thank God for our "Ice Cream Cone Diary."
Paul Hutchens, *My Life and I,* The Sugar Creek Press, Cascade, Colorado, 1962. Used by permission

## THINGS JUST DON'T HAPPEN

Things just don't happen to us who love God,
They're planned by His own dear hand.
Then molded and shaped, and timed by His clock,
Things just don't happen,--they're planned.

We just don't guess on the issues of life,
We Christians just rest in our Lord,
We are directed by His sovereign will,
In the light of His Holy Word.

We who love Jesus are walking by faith,
Not seeing one step that's ahead.
Not doubting one moment what our lot might be,
But looking to Jesus instead.

We praise our dear Savior for loving us so,
For planning each care of our life.
Then giving us faith to trust Him for all,
The blessings as well as the strife.

Things just don't happen to us who love God,
To us who have taken our stand,
No matter the lot, the course, or the price
Things just don't happen, they're planned.

Easter L. Fields

# "THE PROMISE OF GOD"

A True story by Betty Swinford
Pulpit Helps

The following article is one that I clipped out of Pulpit Helps back in the eighties. It brings tears to my eyes every time I read it and I have shared it many times from the pulpit. I remember the third page because I have shared it so many times, so I will write what I do remember

"Roger Simms walked slowly along the highway. He was lean and hard, physically fit. But he was tired, and the suitcase he carried seemed to grow heavier by the minute. He was anxious to get home, see his parents and his girl and get out of his army uniform once and for all.

A new surge of hope gripped him as another car came into view. With a friendly smille, his thumb went back into the air. The hope faded, however, when he realized the car coming toward him was a new sleek black Cadillac.

To his surprise, the car stopped and the passenger door opened for him. He ran toward the car and tossed his suitcase into the back seat.

"Thank you!" he said to the stranger. "Let me tell you, I appreciate this ride."

"Glad to," the other man responded. "Going home for keeps?"

"You bet!" Roger settled back against the plush seat. "I have never in my whole life been so glad to be going home!"

""Well, you are in luck if you are going to Chicago."

"I am not going quite that far." He hesitated while his dark eyes roved the beautiful dash board. "I guess you live in Chicago?"

The other man nodded. "I have a business there. My name is Hanover. Yours?"

"Mr. Simms., Roger Simms."

they talked about many things. Cars, sports, business and life in general. They talked about the war and Roger shared some of his experiences with him.

Then, very quietly, the Holy Spirit spoke to Roger's heart, urging him to witness to Mr. Hanover.

God, I cannot witness to this man about Christ!" he argued silently. "Just look at him! Expensive clothes, fine car, successful business. He would not be interested in spiritual things."

Minutes passed and they chatted some more about impersonal things.

And once more the Spirit of God began to impress Roger too witness to the man who had so kindly given him a ride. And again Roger rebelled. He could not do that! Why, Mr. Hanover would never listen too conversation about Christ! No, he simply could not do it!

Time passed. In another thirty minutes it would be time for Roger to leave Mr. Hanover. The countryside was flying past-the colorful hues of early spring.

The third time the Holy Spirit began speaking to Roger's heart. Urgently He impressed him to speak to Mr. Hanover about his soul. It was an impression Roger could no longer ignore.

He cleared his throat. "Mr. Hanover, I would like to talk to you about something very important. I want to talk toyou about your soul."

Steel gray eyes pierced Roger's dark ones, but he made no reply.

"Sir, I want you to know that Jesus Christ died on the cross in your place. He loved you beyond human limit.

For the next fifteen minutes Roger poured out his soul.

He explained the way of salvation and ultimately asked if Mr. Hanover would not like too receive Christ as his Savior.

To Roger's astonishment, the Cadillac stopped bedside he road. He wondered if Mr. Hanover had had enough and was about to dump him. Instead, the businessman bowed his head over the steering wheel of the car and began weeping. Brokenly he wept his way to Christ.

A few minutes later he dropped Roger in front of his home. "Thank you, Roger. This is the greatest thing that has ever happened to me." He fished for his wallet and brought out a small white business card. "This is where you can find me if you are ever in Chicago."

Nothing could compare to his joy, that this day he had won a soul to Christ! Oh, it was great to be home again. The dinner his mother had prepared was wonderful. Spending the evening with his girl was ecstatic. But Mr. Hanover had been born again. That was more important than anything else in the world.

In a few months Roger and Beth were married and in two years a little son was born. He started his own business and God began to bless it.

Then one morning he learned that he must go to Chicago. He dug out a suitcase and began to pack. When he reached into a drawer for some socks, his fingers encountered the small white business card given to him five years before by Mr. Hanover.

A smile lighted Roger's countenance. Why not? He would be right there inthe city. Why not look up Mr. Hanover and see how he was getting along?

It was on a Tuesday morning. The sting of the first snow was in the air and the steam from various factories hung in the air like great ghostly apparitions. Roger

stepped inside the pretentious doors of the Hanover Enterprises .A receptionist sat at a desk in the plush room before him.
I am Roger Simms. I would like very much to see Mr. Hanover."
A strange look came over the young woman's face. "That is not possible, Mr. Simms."
Roger felt confused. "I am sure he will remember me. I am the hitchhiker he picked up one afternoon five years ago.
The receptionist was unyielding. Then, "Perhaps you would like to talk to Mrs. Hanover?"
Roger was more puzzled than ever. "I don't know Mrs. Hanover, but—yes, of course, that will be fine." Apparently that was the only way he would find out just what was going on.
A quick message was given over the intercom and then, "Come this way, please, Mr. Simms."
Almost immediately Roger was face to face with a keen-eyed woman in her mid-fifties. She extended her hand. "You knew my husband?"
Roger sat down across from her. "Yes. He picked me up when I was on my way home from the war."
"Can you tell me just when that was? I mean, what day?"

[This is where I have to finish the story.]
He gave the date and she began to cry.
She said, "My husband never made it home, because on that day he was killed in a car wreck."
She reasoned that Roger Simms had been sent by God to witness to him. in answer to her prayers and Mr. Hanover had invited Jesus Christ into his life. God had answered her prayer and she would see him in heaven.

# WHEN SOMETHING BREAKS
April 2004

A member of a church where I served gave me a book entitled *DON'T SWEAT THE SMALL STUFF* and it's all small stuff by Richard Carlson, Ph.D. (Hyperion, New York). It contained a hundred thought provoking articles two to three pages long, which gave me food for thought.

One particular article was entitled "See the Glass as Already Broken (and Everything Else Too)". He brought out the fact that everything is in a state of change. Just like our washing machines, cars, VCRs, clothes, dishes— whatever is created in our modern world will eventually break.

He brought out a thought, that rather than being surprised or disappointed when it breaks, expect it to break sometime—enjoy it while you have it and it's working.

He used our favorite drinking glass as an illustration. Use the glass and put into it whatever you enjoy drinking. He said to imagine it as already broken in the future and enjoy it while you have it, but know someday it probably will get broken.

Someone might say: "What a pessimistic attitude!" but I don't think it is. How many times have we enjoyed the wonderful trips our car has provided, but one day it breaks down. Rather than go to pieces, remember the wonderful times we had in it, but it finally got to the place where it needed a repair or we needed a new car.

This isn't a new idea. The wisest man that ever lived, other than Jesus Christ, said the same thing in a book he wrote. His name was Solomon. In chapter 3 of Ecclesiastes he wrote:

To everything *there is* a season,

A time for every purpose under heaven:

2  A time to be born,
And a time to die;
A time to plant,
And a time to pluck *what is* planted;

3  A time to kill,
And a time to heal;
A time to break down,
And time to build up;

4  A time to weep,
And a time to laugh;
A time to mourn,
And a time to dance;

5  A time to cast away stones,
And a time to gather stones;
A time to embrace,
And a time to refrain from embracing;

6  A time to gain,
And a time to lose;
A time to keep,
And a time to throw away;

7  A time to tear,
And a time to sew;
A time to keep silence,
And a time to speak;

8  A time to love,
And a time to hate;
A time of war,
And a time of peace. NKJV

I know that sometimes I get frustrated when something breaks—whether it's some electrical appliance, or my car, but I need to enjoy it while I can use it.

This carries through also with friendships. Dr. Jack Smith, a missionary to Uganda and a close friend, shared with me one time that friendships are like two boats floating parallel down the river and sometimes one of the boats takes another course and the friendship parts. The key thing is to enjoy the friendship while we have it. In the future, because of circumstances, one of the parties may go in another direction in life after a season has passed.

Solomon's words about life fit here too about our daily life. When my father who was dying of cancer, told me that he and mom were enjoying one day at a time because they knew the time would come when Dad would go to be with Jesus and they wanted to enjoy each day to the fullest..

The psalmist wrote: *This is the day the LORD has made; let us rejoice and be glad in it.* Psalm 118:24. We need to be thankful for each day and enjoy it to its fullest.

# FAKE FLOWERS

My father is an interesting character. At age 86, he loves to grow things in his yard. He has a small vegetable garden and flowers everywhere. But there's a strange bush near his front door that draws a lot of attention. It has white and yellow blooms, red ones, blue ones, purple, and green. Dad takes silk and plastic flowers and wires them onto the bush alongside the real ones. I told you he was a character! People visiting our home will often stare at that sight. Some of them even ask for a cutting from it.

I tell the children in our church that one sign you are growing into maturity is when you know what's real and what's not. Many adults have trouble with this. Some spend their lives chasing the fake and imaginary as though it actually had meaning.

God once told a very young Jeremiah, "If you learn to extract the precious from the worthless, you shall be as my mouth." (cf. Jeremiah 15:19). That is,, His prophet. This skill of discernment means three things. First there is knowing the difference in what's of value and what is junk. Second is leaving the worthless alone, and the third skill is selecting the valuable.

This is all about the choices we make everyday—the use of our time (should we watch TV or help a neighbor?), the books we read (trash or edifying), the dollars we spend (impulse items or something worthwhile), the food we eat, the friends we choose, our schools, careers and life decisions.                    Joe McKeever, *Christian Clippings*

# INSIGNIFICANT?
June 2005

I had a Christian leader visit the church I am pastoring. After the service, as we were talking, he asked a question that I have been pondering ever since.

The question was this: Who has led more people to accept Jesus Christ as their Savior in our time than anyone else? I suggested Billy Graham, but he said there was another person who has been responsible for more people to be saved.

He said he didn't know the man's name, but he was the man who led Billy Graham to the Lord who would in future years lead thousands to the Lord.

I did some research and found there were two men involved in Dr. Graham's conversion. Dr Mordecai Ham held evangelistic meetings in Charlotte, North Carolina. Billy went down the aisle in one of those meetings to accept Christ when the invitation was given. The second man was an insignificant tailor named J. E. Prevatt, who was a friend of the family. He stepped up beside Billy at the altar, put his arms around him and urged him to make his decision. He explained God's plan for Billy's salvation in a simple way and Billy committed his life to Christ.

The second example is an insignificant person who led Charles Spurgeon to the Lord. Charles Haddon Spurgeon became a great preacher a century ago.

The story of his conversion is wonderful to read. The internet has a vast amount of information about Charles Spurgeon. But the point I want to make is that in a little church one snowy Sunday morning when  the pastor couldn't get to church to preach, an insignificant common man was chosen to preach. He only used one Bible verse and kept repeating it, Isaiah 45:22, and God used the insignificant man to touch the heart of that 16 year old boy to invite Christ into his life. Little did he realize that boy would become a great preacher in London who would preach to thousands, have his sermons read all over the world and accomplish His purpose.

He used common, insignificant fishermen, and a tax collector to be His disciples.

He used me, an insignificant pastor, to have the great privilege to serve as a mentor to three young men who were training for the ministry. The Bible school that I graduated from had become a seminary and set up a two year mentor program with local pastors who would give pastoral students experience working with a pastor.

I jumped at the opportunity to become a mentor and volunteered to be in the program to spend quality time with a student sharing myself and my ministry with him. I had pastored three churches and was able to give him experience in preaching, visitation, teaching, sharing myself with him in all areas of the ministry.during the two year period he would be with me. What a blessing it was to have a part in their future ministry. One of the men, Scott Benner, has kept in touch with me during the years and he has become a verfy successful pastor in Maine.

The reason I have shared this experience in my life is that I was serving in a medium sized church which wasn't significant to some people, but God was gracious to give me an opportuniuty to be a mentor . Scot Benner has reached many who have become Christians who have reached others, and on and on it goes.multiplying souls saved.

You may feel like an insignificant Christian, but God uses insignificant believers to reach those who are without Christ. All God asks you to do is to be available and willing to share.

# A NEW NORMAL
September 2008

I came across this personal testimony of a family that lost their Marine son in Iraq. I think your heart will be touched by what the father wrote.

"With Jesse, our Marine son, in Iraq, we knew precisely what it meant when two Marines in dress blues came to our door. Somehow, we survived hearing them tell us that our son had been killed in action. God graciously held us in His arms as we dealt with the initial shock, called our other two children to tell them the news, and endured our first night of grief.

Thus began the process that would forever change the way we dealt with life. We rode the emotional rollercoaster that was the media onslaught, the comfort of friends, the memorial service, the paper work, and our bodies' physical responses, while trying to keep up with the everyday things of bills, jobs and housework. It was an emotional jumble of blessings and sorrows that made each new day a new challenge. We are still learning to cope.

Following a traumatic occurrence such as this, it is intuitively obvious to those involved that nothing will ever be the same again, that there will forever be a new normal. We have to realize that things won't ever be as though nothing has happened. People around us also have to decipher how to relate to our situation, wanting to help without hurting. The result is confusion and unexpected stress, both internally and in our relationships.

Things that seemed very important before, are now insignificant. Things that seemed trival before, take on new, often overwhelming, significance, which may or may not be understood by those around us. For example, when someone around me speaks of thinking they should spend more time with their children, I have a passionate response that I have to fight to control. I want to shout, "Do it now!"

Everywhere I go, everywhere I look, I see things that move me, reminding me of my son. They are all good memories, as that is the way he was, but they also remind me of my loss, and that's tough on my heart. I'll never escape them, don't want to, but I have to figure out how to process them properly.

The problem is that you are moving into unknown territory for which you have no training or experience. And most of the people who offer advice have no training or experience either. They always have good intentions, but can only tell you what they think they would do in that situation. So you are on your own, and the resulting actions and reactions aren't weird, but new normal, to be evaluated and revised as time goes on, but not to be feared or to be worried about.

Last week they brought us our son's things from Iraq. Now what do we do with different reactions to each item? It felt nice to have things of his, but hard to have them remind us of our loss. His watch seemed particularly comforting as he was wearing it that night. Then the alarm went off at 11 pm Iraqi time, the time he awoke for his appointment with destiny. Welcome to new normal.

So if I wear my son's lapel chevrons, and people mistakenly assume that I'm doing that to keep him near or to give me chances to talkabout him, that's okay. I actually wear them because it steadies me somehow and that's not wrong. It's new normal and I have no idea why it does that or how long it still do that. It just helps for now, whether others understand or not.

New normal includes a variety of new experiences. There are the unexpected tears at inopportune times. There is forgetfulness that leaves you wandering in a daze.

At times you can't decide what to have, as the waiter stands at your table. And that's just the start.

Not to worry. People will wait while you dry your tears. Post-it notes can keep you on track. Waiters are paid to be polite in any situation. You find yourself in a period of grace while you're finding new normal.

Then there's the traumatic occurrence itself. People tend to tip-toe around it, unsure of what to say or what to do. It's a learning time for everybody involved. We found it helped to talk about things, especially with people who were understanding. Those who were patient and willing to talk about our son and his death helped us learn to cope.

Your relationship with the world has also changed. New patterns of fitting in have to be learned, and people have to figure out how to relate to you in your new setting, as well. Others have to keep on with their lives while you are still trying to deal with your trauma. It's like dropping out of a hiking party to explore, and look up to find the group has moved on, and you now have to catch up to rejoin them. Except, in this situation, it is kind of hard to yell, "Wait up!"

Another factor in new normal is the establishment of a new identity. For years to come I will be viewed by others as the father different person than I was before, but it's as though I've been set aside as a monument to my son for others to salute as they go by. As the world goes on around me, I'm trying to discover how I can rejoin the human race, sort of like getting on a moving of the Marine who died tragically in Iraq. I don't feel like a merry-go-round.

Thankfully, Jesus is the constant, the solid rock, of my new normal. Jesus, who died for me, Jesus, who said, "I will not leave you comfortless. I will come to you."

Jesus, who promised, "I will never leave you or forsake you." What an anchor He has been.

When, as a teenager, I gave my life to Jesus, He also gave his life to me, to be all that I will ever need. No day is too hard for Him, no matter how difficult it is for me. No puzzle is too confusing for Him, no matter how confused I am. He will always be there, walking each step of the way with me, ready to listen to the cry of my heart. His Word instructs me and settles my thoughts. His Spirit guides me, comforts and teaches me. His power gives me calm assurance that I will find new normal and will be able to function successfully again.

Below are some Scripture passages that have helped me along the road toward new normal. I share them with the hope that they will encourage you, too.

**This verse is the awesome foundation of the living hope I have.**

*Blessed be the God and Father of our Lord Jesus Christ, which according to His abundant mercy has begotten us again with a loving hope by the resurrection of Jesus Christ from the dead."* 1 Peter 1:3

**These verses not only comfort me but help me with understanding some of the purpose of my heartache:**

*"Blessed be God, even the Father of our Lord Jesus Christ, the Father of mercies, and the God of all comfort;*
*Who comforts us in all our tribulation, that we may be able to comfort them which are in any trouble, by the comfort wherewith we ourselves are comforted by God."*
2 Corinthians 1:3-4
*"Yea, though I walk through the valley of the shadow of death, I will fear no evil:, for thou art with me. Thy rod and Thy staff they comfort me."*Psalm 23:4

So, that's what I've been thinking about, trying to cope with a different world, working toward new normal. If you'd like to talk about Jesse, or about a traumatic occurrence of your own, please feel free to contact us. We'd be glad to talk with you. God bless you."
Nathan & Vicki Strong10.5
1367 Creek Road
IRASBURG VT 05845 (802)754-2790
victonasstrong@juno.com

SGT. JESSE STRONG

# WONDERFUL COUNSELOR

December 2007

Back in the Old Testament, the prophet Isaiah prophesied about the coming Messiah who would be God in the flesh. (Isaiah 7:14; 9:6; John 1:14). He gave four names that would characterize this person: *Wonderful Counselor, Mighty God, Everlasting Father, Prince of Peace.* (Isaiah 9:6, 7). These names would be known by some, but the majority of those living in that day when He entered the world would not know Him—in fact, they would reject Him and put Him on a cross.

Today we know that person was the Lord Jesus Christ who came and was born in Bethlehem 2,000 years ago, and we will celebrate His coming to earth during this month of December.

His name, Wonderful Counselor, is a beautiful name and it holds so much significance to those who are His followers.

A couple got to meet Him before He came into the world as a human being. The husband's name was Manoah. You can read about the angel of the Lord appearing in Judges 13 when He told Manoah and his wife they would have a child who they would name Samson. When asked what the angel of the Lord's name was, He said it was "Wonderful" (Judges 13:18), and in the Hebrew it means "a miracle, something amazing, a wonder, beyond understanding." After the Angel of the Lord left, Manoah said to his wife, "We have seen God!" Truly our Lord is beyond understanding and His birth was a miracle as well as the miracles He performed on earth.

The second part of His name is Counselor, in the Hebrew meaning "to advise, to deliberate, resolve,

45

determine, guide." Putting them together we come up with the fact He is a *Wonderful Counselor*.

There may be times in our lives when we need to consult a professional Christian counselor who can help us get ourselves back on track in our life. I know there was a time in my life when I needed a Christian counselor and it has helped me in my counseling as a pastor. But the greatest counselor is Jesus Christ Himself.

As I thought about His name, *Wonderful Counselor*, I thought how Jesus Christ is a Wonderful Counselor in my life and in the believer's life. Jesus Christ as a Wonderful Counselor performs the following in a believer's life.

First of all, He wants me to start where I am and to admit that I have a need for help. I have to recognize that sin has separated me from God and that it is only through Him that I can be saved. Jesus said, "For God so loved the world that He gave His one and only Son, that whoever believes in Him shall not perish, but have everlasting life." (John 3:16)

•Secondly, after I have chosen Him to be my Savior and counselor, He wants me to trust Him as my counselor. The words He spoke to His disciples the night He was betrayed so fit this thought when He gave the encouraging words, "Let not your heart be troubled: ye believe in God, believe also in me." (John 14:1) As my Counselor, He knows about my life before I share it with him. In Psalm 139 David declared God knows where I am, my thoughts before I speak, knows where I am going, knew me before I was born, has a plan for my life and has every day recorded in His book.

•He has the wisdom to direct my life—how to deal with problems I am facing. Proverbs 3:5, 6 states, "Trust in the Lord with all your heart and lean not on your own understanding; in all your ways submit to him and he will make your paths straight." NIV' We see crises at home and abroad—domestic crises in our own nation—international crises in our world each night on our television sets. We individually suffer from frustration, confusion seeking for answers in the mixed up world that we are living in, and He gives guidance, leadership and direction in our life.

⚫As my counselor, He will help me to understand others and to love those around me. His great commandment is, "A new command I give you: Love one another. As I have loved you, so you must love one another. By this everyone will know that you are my disciples, if you love one another." (John 13:34, 35 NIV)

⚫Being my counselor He wants me to spend time with Him. His desire is expressed when he said, "Come to me, all you who are weary and burdened, and I will give you rest. Take my yoke upon you and learn from me, for I am gentle and humble in heart, and you will find rest for your souls. For my yoke is easy and my burden is light." (Matthew 11:28-30)

⚫He knows my counseling will be a long process—the rest of my life--and will go with me every step I will take. "Never will I leave you; never will I forsake you." (Hebrews 13:5; Deuteronomy 31:6)

⚫Lastly, He wants me to apply what I have learned in my counseling with Him in my life. "'Jesus answered and said unto him, 'If a man love me, he will keep my words: and my Father will love him, and we will come unto him, and make our abode with him. '" (John 14:23)

As our *Wonderful Counselor* He truly is *The Prince of Peace* to our soul and in our life.


BIBLE VERSE: JOHN 14:1`

## WHAT ABOUT BOB?

A friend of mine told me about someone that drove him crazy. His name was Bob. My friend was grumbling about Bob under his breath, and God was listening

That night everything changed because God spoke to him as clearly as He had ever spoken before. God said, "You know that fellow, Bob, who is a little slow and never quite gets things right? The one you avoid at all costs? Well, I want you to remember something—compared to Me, you are not the sharpest knife in the drawer, either, and you don't get things quite right most of the time. So, the next time Bob starts to bug you, remember you're My Bob."

My own Bob was a lady who rode the van to our church. When I had important things to do, I would try to sneak by without her seeing me. She always saw me and would yell, "Pastor, good morning!"

After church we greeted guests in the Hospitality Room and she always came in to give me a hug. I hugged her, and I enjoyed it. Because I know she was my Bob, I knew that in her simplistic mind, I represented God. God in His still, small voice said, "Well done, Charles. You loved someone who needed my love desperately. When you are desperate for love, I'll be there for you like you were for her." And when I was desperate, He was there.

I have now resigned from that church and when I look back on my time there, she is one of the people I miss. Why? Because I know she really needed me. I prayed that God would send her another Charles—and me another Bob, and give me enough sense to recognize him when he shows up.

J.A.Gillmartin,Sheepcribone,blogstop.com, quoted in
*Pulpit Helps,* published by AMG Publishers, Chattanooga, TN 37421

# HOW CAN GOD USE ME?

January 2004

*[Note: Gladys was 85 years old when I interviewed her in 2004 before she went to meet her Lord a few years later. I am sure the Lord said when she arrived in heaven, "Well done thou good and faithful servant,"]*

Gladys Gassoway is a former pastor's wife. Her husband was the preceding pastor before I became the pastor at Skyline Baptist in North Bend, Oregon, where I served for 20 years. Her husband had passed away. Gladys found a special ministry that has touched many people. Through the years I have continued to keep in touch with her. She is now 85 years old, but that hasn't stopped her from being a tool that the Lord could use.

Gladys' ministry consists of calling 70-75 people each night and singing a song to them, depending on how many are at home. She starts early in the evening at 6:30 and continues until she sings to the last one between 10:30 to 11 p.m. The call lasts between 5 to 10 minutes. It is a special ministry. The oldest person she sings to is 105 years old. During the week she touches in totall 110 people. Some she sings to once or twice during the week and others each night.

When she first started her ministry, to the people she sang to, the youngest was four and full of excitement and now she is in her teens.

She has a personal interest in each one. There are times when the person on the other end of the line may be sick, or has a special need and Gladys has an opportunity to listen and to pray for them. She has a theme each month such as *praise* during January, and *love* during February. and chooses songs to go with that theme as well as shares a Scripture with them  All denominations are represented by those she sings to.

Gladys lets the Lord use her to minister to those around her.  She remarked to me that some have wanted to do what she does, but they are not consistent each night because things interfere or interrupt.  She makes sure that every night those who have requested it get their phone call with a special song for them.

The strength and success of my ministry has been the prayer support of a great group of people, Gladys included. Only recently I had the opportunity to be the interim pastor for a year and experienced God's blessing as I saw God's manifold blessing in the work there.  I had several who said, "I'm praying for you."...

The Apostle Paul recognized the need of intercessory prayer on his part when he wrote to the Christians at Ephesus and  shared:  *[18]praying always with all prayer and supplication in the Spirit, being watchful to this end with all severance and supplication for all the saints—.* (Ephesians 6:18)

There was a lady by the name of Dorcas in the town of Joppa when the Apostle Peter was doing his ministry.  She did a ministry of helping the poor by sewing robes and other clothing  She was faithful using the ability that God had blessed her with. (Acts 9:39)

Gladys shared with me that sometimes people say: "God has never told me to do something." But Gladys says: "Did you ever listen?"

Maybe God has something special for you to do this year.  Maybe it is being a special prayer warrior, an encourager, or another special ministry God wants you to do. Gladys listened--are you listening?

# GOD LIVES UNDER THE BED
October 2007'

[Note: Here's an article that I came across this last month in the *Exchange*. I really enjoyed reading it and I think it has some lessons for all of us to learn.]

I envy Kevin. My brother Kevin thinks God lives under his bed. At least that's what I heard him say one night. He was praying out loud in his dark bedroom, and I stopped to listen. "Are you there, God?" he said. "Where are you? Oh, I see. Under the bed…"

I giggled softly and tiptoed off to my room. Kevin's unique perspectives are often a source of amusement. But that night something else lingered long after the humor. I realized for the first time the very different world Kevin lives in.

He was born 30 years ago, mentally disabled as a result of difficulties during labor. Apart from his size (he's 6'2") there are few ways in which he is an adult.

He reasons and communicates with the capabilities of a 7 year old, and he always will. He will probably always believe that God lives under his bed, that Santa Clause is the one who fills the space under our tree every Christmas and that airplanes stay up in the sky because angels carry them.

I remember wondering if Kevin realizes he is different.
ever dissatisfied with his monotonous life?

Up before dawn each day, off to work at a workshop for the disabled, home to walk our cocker spaniel, return to eat his favorite macaroni and cheese for dinner and later to bed.

The only variation in the entire scheme is laundry, when he hovers excitedly over the washing machine like a mother with her newborn child.

He does not seem dissatisfied.

He lopes out to the bus every morning at 7:05, eager for a day of simple work.

He wrings his hands excitedly while the water boils on the stove before dinner, and he stays up late twice a week to gather our dirty laundry for his next day's laundry chores.

And Saturdays, oh the bliss of Saturdays! That's the day my Dad takes Kevin to the airport to have a soft drink, watch the planes land, and speculate loudly on the destination of each passenger inside.

"That one's goin' to Chi-car-go!" Kevin shouts as he claps his hands.

His anticipation is so great he can hardly sleep on Friday nights.

And so goes his world of daily rituals and weekend field trips.

He doesn't know what it means to be discontented.

His life is simple.

He will never know the entanglements of wealth or power and he does not care what brand of clothing he wears or what kind of food he eats. His needs have always been met, and he never worries that one day they may not be.

His hands are diligent. Kevin is never so happy as when he is working. When he unloads the dishwasher or vacuums the carpet, his heart is completely in it.

He does not shrink from a job when it is begun, and he does not leave a job until it is finished. But when his tasks are done, Kevin knows how to relax.

He is not obsessed with his work or the work of others. His heart is pure.

He still believes everyone tells the truth, promises must be kept, and when you are wrong, you apologize instead of argue.

Free from pride an unconcerned with appearances, Kevin is not afraid to cry when he is hurt, angry or sorry. He is always transparent, always sincere. And he trusts God.

Not confined by intellectual reasoning, when he comes to Christ, he comes as a child. Kevin seems to know God, to really be friends with Him in a way that is difficult for an "educated" person to grasp. God seems like his closest companion.

In my moments of doubt and frustrations with my Christianity, I envy the security Kevin has in his simple faith.

It is then that I am most willing to admit that he has some divine knowledge that rises above my mortal questions.

It is then I realize that perhaps he is not the one with the handicap…I am. My obligations, my fear, my pride, my circumstances; they all become disabilities when I do not trust them to God's care.

Who knows if Kevin comprehends things I can never learn? After all, he has spent his whole life in that kind of innocence, praying after dark and soaking up the goodness and love of God.

And one day, when the mysteries of heaven are opened, and we are all amazed at how close God really is to our hearts, I'll realize that God heard the simple prayers of a boy who believed that God lived under his bed.

Kevin won't be surprised at all!

Author Unknown ' The Exchange,

REMEMBER, TIM AND LAUREN—
EVEN IF YOUR MARRIAGE IS MADE
IN HEAVEN, THE MAINTENANCE
WORK IS DONE HERE ON EARTH.

# TEACH ME LORD TO WAIT
September 2007

One of the hardest words for me to apply to my life is the verb *to wait*. I am an "A" personality and I like to see things done yesterday, or drive myself to complete a task today. My wife says I'm always busy doing projects. Learning to wait is an area God has worked on and continues to work on in my life to teach me the importance of learning to *wait*.

At the present time it has been exceedingly hard to adjust to patiently wait for my strength to come back after having a heart *attack* on April 1st. It's taking time going through a rehabilitation program three times a week to build up my heart so that I might gain strength.

Having a heart attack has changed my life and has caused me to ponder what God has ahead for me in my life as His child. God has extended my life and it is important for me to not rush ahead of Him, but to patiently wait on Him to direct my path.

There is a passage of Scripture written by Isaiah who shares with those in Israel who were having a time of waiting on God. Isaiah, being led by God, instructs in the following verses what he learned about waiting on God. *7Why do you say, O Jacob, and complain, O Israel, "My way is hidden from the LORD; my cause is disregarded by my God"?*

*28Do you not know? Have you not heard? The LORD is the everlasting God the Creator of the ends of the earth. He will not grow tired or weary, and his understanding no one can fathom*

. *29 He gives strength to the weary and increases the power of the weak. 30Even youths grow tired and weary, and young men stumble and fall;*
*31but those who hope (wait, who expect, look for and hope in Him Amplified Bible) in the LORD will renew their*  *strength. They will soar on wings like eagles; they will run and not grow weary, they will walk and not be faint.* (Isaiah 40:27-31 NIV)

What does Isaiah share that we can apply to our lives about learning from God how to wait upon Him?

First of all, Isaiah shares God is personal, *"my God."* God isn't a God way out there, but is very close to each one who knows Him. Solomon wrote, *" there is a friend that sticks closer than a brother",* in speaking about the Lord. (Proverbs 18:24) He is also a Father who cares about His children. Jesus said, *"Look at the birds of the air; they do not sow or reap or store away in barns, and yet your heavenly Father feeds them. Are you not much more valuable than they?"* ( Matthew 6:26 NIV)

Secondly, God has attributes. *The LORD is the everlasting God the Creator of the ends of the earth. He will not grow tired or weary, and his understanding no one can fathom.*(Isaiah 40:28 NIV) Being eternal He knows what is up ahead because He knows the end from the beginning. He is the Creator and He can surely help the created. He has unlimited strength and never faints nor is weary, so He's available all the time. He never errs in what He does because His understanding no one can fathom. He knows what is best for us.

Thirdly, He empowers our lives as we go through this journey of life. If we *wait, expect, look for and hope in Him,* Isaiah gives the results: *He gives strength to the weary and increases the power of the weak. Even youths grow tired and weary, and young men stumble and fall.* (Isaiah 40:29 NIV)

Isaiah then gives the results in our life when we wait upon the LORD.

1. We will soar on wings like eagles. As the eagle experiences in flight freedom and perspective of what is below, so trusting God will give us freedom and heavenly perspective to what is happening in our life.

2. We will run and not be weary or exhausted. When God gives us strength to wait, we won't become exhausted or impatient because we trust in Him. Running also speaks of a goal and we will achieve our goals by waiting on the Lord.

3. We shall walk, but not faint. The Christian life is called a **walk. It is one step after another, and it means committing our daily life to the Lord's direction in our life.**

"F. B. Meyer, the great preacher of yesteryear, stated:

'Never act in a panic, nor allow man to dictate to you, calm yourself and be still; force yourself into the quiet of your closet until the pulse beats normally and the 'scare' has ceased to disturb. When you are most eager to act is the time when you will make the most pitiable mistakes. Do not say in your heart what you will or will not do, but WAIT UPON GOD until He makes known His way. So long as that way is hidden, it is clear that there is no need of action, and that He accounts Himself responsible for all results of keeping you where you are.'" Quoted in Our Daily Bread, Radio Bible Class Ministries, Grand Rapids, Michigan.

I need to remember and you do too, that God has a plan for our lives and we need to trust Him to work it out in His time. Like I said, I have a tendency to be impatient with God working in my life. Teach me Lord to wait!

But they that wait upon the LORD shall renew *their* strength; they shall mount up with wings as eagles; they shall run, and not be weary; *and* they shall walk, and not faint.

**Isaiah 40:31**

# CARING LOVE
February 2008

This month could be called the love month because we celebrate Valentines Day on February 14th. The shelves of our stores are full of special boxes of candy, and stuffed animals bearing the message, "I Love You". Florists are busy advertising special flower bouquets and jewelers feature special jewelry for the one you love and on it goes.

There is a passage of Scripture that is very special to me that illustrates a special love being demonstrated to our Lord and Savior Jesus Christ by a woman who was named Mary. Our Lord says these words that are recorded by three of the Gospel writers about her:

"I tell you the truth, wherever this gospel is preached throughout the world, what she has done will also be told in memory of her." (Matt. 26:10-13; Mark 14:3-9; John 12:1-7).

Who was this Mary and what did she do that so affected our Lord that He spoke these words about her?

Mary appears in three incidents in the New Testament. The first appearance of her name is at the home where she, her sister Martha, and her brother Lazarus lived located in Bethany. (Luke 10:38-42) The Lord was visiting this family and it is recorded that she was at the feet of Jesus before they ate listening to Jesus teach.

We read her sister, Martha, was upset because Mary wasn't helping her get the meal ready but was listening to what Jesus was saying sitting at His feet. When Martha complained, Jesus replied that only one thing is needed and Mary has chosen what is better, and it will not be taken away from her." (Luke 10:41,42) Mary was listening to Jesus' teaching.

The second passage of Scripture records that her brother Lazarus died and Jesus had waited four days before going to Bethany to be with Mary and Martha. Martha met him outside the town but Mary stayed at home waiting for Jesus to arrive. John 11:1-43

- When Mary heard that Jesus had arrived, she quickly went to Him outside of town. We read "When Mary reached the place where Jesus was and saw him, she fell at his feet and said, 'Lord, if you had been here, my brother would not have died.'"

We read that Jesus was deeply moved in His spirit and troubled when He saw Mary and the Jews with her weeping and asked where had they laid Lazarus' body. The shortest verse in the Bible is recorded, "Jesus wept." (John 11:35) The reaction of the Jews was, "See how he loved him!" (Lazarus) Jesus then has them remove the stone from the tomb where Lazarus is buried. Jesus says a prayer to the Father and then with a loud voice calls, "Lazarus come forth" and he appeared in grave clothes having risen from death.

The third appearance of Mary's name is six days before Jesus was killed. Jesus arrived at Bethany and attended a dinner at the home of a man called Simon the Leper. (Matt. 26:6-13; Mark 14:3-9; John 12:1-8). The account follows as recorded by Matthew: 26:6-12

6Now when Jesus was in Bethany, in the house of Simon the leper, 7There came unto him a woman having an alabaster box of very precious ointment, and poured it on his head, as he sat *at meat*. 8But when his disciples saw *it*, they had indignation, saying, To what purpose *is* this waste? 9For this ointment might have been sold for much, and given to the poor. 10When Jesus understood *it*, he said unto them, Why trouble ye the woman? for she hath I say unto you, Wheresoever this gospel shall be preached in the whole world, *there* shall also this, that this woman hath done, be told for a memorial of her. Mary wrought a good work upon me. [11]For ye have the poor always with you; but me ye have not always. [12]For in that she hath poured this ointment on my body, she did *it* for my burial. (Matthew 26:6-12)

From my study of Scripture, Mary was the only one who comprehended Jesus' prediction that He would be crucified. He had told His disciples time and time again what would happen but they hadn't grasped it. Mary is the only one who listened, sitting at His feet, to what He had said before it happened and loved her Lord so much she let Him know she realized what lay before Him.

Mary is an example of what true love involves. It involves listening to the other person and showing them that you care. This is one of the greatest gifts of love you can show another person. Think about it this month when someone shares something dear to their heart. They will remember that you cared enough to listen.

BIBLE VERSE: JOHN 13:34, 35

## When You Thought I Wasn't Looking

When you thought I wasn't looking, I saw you hang my first painting on the refrigerator, and I immediately wanted to paint another one.

When you thought I wasn't looking, I saw you feed a stray cat, and I learned that it was good to be kind to animals.

When you thought I wasn't looking, I saw you make my favorite cake for me, and I learned that the little things can be the special things in life.

When you thought I wasn't looking, I heard you say a prayer, and I knew that there was a God I could talk to, and I learned to trust God.

When you thought I wasn't looking, I saw you make a meal and take it to a friend who was sick, and I learned that we all have to help take care of each other.

When you thought I wasn't looking, I saw you give of your time and money to help people who had nothing, and I learned that those who have something should give to those who don't.

When you thought I wasn't looking, I felt you kiss me good night, and I felt loved and safe.

When you thought I wasn't looking, I saw you take care of our house and everyone in it, and I learned to take care of what we are given.

When you thought I wasn't looking, I saw how you handled your responsibilities, even though you didn't feel good, and I learned that I would have to be responsible when I grew up.

When you thought I wasn't looking, I saw tears come from your eyes, and I learned that sometimes things hurt, but it's all right to cry.

When you thought I wasn't looking, I saw that you cared, and I wanted to be everything that I could be.

When you thought I wasn't looking, I learned most of life's lessons that I need to know to be a good and productive person when I grow up.

When you thought I wasn't looking, I looked at you and wanted to say, "Thanks for the things I saw … when you thought I wasn't looking.                    The Exchange,

# "INFORMATION PLEASE"
### February 2005

{I love this story that appeared in *Christian Clippings*]

When I was quite young, my father had one of the first telephones in our neighborhood. I remember well, the polished old case fastened to the wall and the shiny receiver on the side of the box.

I was too little to reach the telephone, but used to listen with fascination when my mother would talk to it. Then I discovered that somewhere inside the wonderful device lived an amazing person and her name was "Information Please" and there was nothing she did not know. "Information Please" could supply anybody's number and the correct time.

My first personal experience with this genie-in-a-bottle came one day while my mother was visiting a neighbor. Amusing myself at the tool bench in the basement, I whacked my finger with a hammer. The pain was terrible but there didn't seem to be any reason in crying because there was no one home to give me sympathy. I walked around the house sucking my throbbing finger, finally arriving at the stairway—The telephone!

Quickly, I ran for the footstool in the parlor, climbed up, took the receiver and held it to my ear, "Information Please" I said into the mouthpiece just above my head.

"Information."

"I hurt my finger!" I wailed into the phone. The tears came readily enough now that I had an audience.

"Isn't your mother home?" came the question.

"Nobody's home but me," I blubbered.

"Are you bleeding?" the voice asked.

"No," I replied. "I hit my finger with a hammer and it hurts."

"Can you open your icebox?" she asked. I said I could. "Then chip off a piece of ice and hold it to your finger," said the voice.

After that, I called "Information Please" for everything. I asked her to help with my geography and she told where Philadelphia was. She helped me with my math. She told me that my pet chipmunk, which I had caught in the park just the day before, would eat fruit and nuts.

Then there was the time Peter, our pet canary died. I called "Information Please? And told her the sad story. She listened, then said the usual thing grown-ups say to soothe a child. But, I was inconsolable. I asked her, "Why is it that birds should sing so beautifully and bring joy to all families, only to end up as a heap of feathers on the bottom of a cage?"

She must have sensed my deep concern, for she said quietly, "Paul, you must remember that there are other worlds to sing in. " Somehow, I felt better.

Another day I was on the telephone. "Information please."

"Information," said the now familiar voice. "How do you spell fix!" I asked.

All this took place in a small town in the Pacific Northwest. When I was nine years old, we moved across the country to Boston. I missed my friend very much. "Information Please" belonged in that old wooden box phone that sat on the table in the hall.

As I grew into my teens, the memories of those childhood conversations never really left me. Often in moments of doubt and perplexity I would recall the serene sense of security I had then. I appreciated now how patient, understanding and kind she was to have spent her time on a little boy.

A few years later, on my way west to college, my plane put down in Seattle. I had about half-an-hour or so between planes. I spent 15 minutes or so on the phone with my sister, who lived there now. Then, without thinking about what I was doing, I dialed my hometown operator and said, "Information Please." Miraculously, I heard the small clear voice I knew so well.

"Information.

I hadn't planned this, but I heard myself saying, "Could you please tell me how to spell fix?"    There was a long pause. Then came the soft spoken answer, "I guess your finger must be healed by now."

I laughed, "So it's really still you." I said. "I wonder if you have any idea how much you meant to me during that time?"

"I wonder," she said, "if you know how much your calls meant to me. I never had any children and I used to look forward to your calls." I told her how often I had thought of her over the years and asked if I could call her again when I came back to visit my sister.

"Please do," she said. "Just ask for Sally."

Three months later I was back in Seattle. A different voice answered, "Information."

I asked for Sally. "Are you a friend," she said.

"Yes, a very old fried," I answered. "I'm sorry to have to tell you this," she said. "Sally had been working part time in the last few years because she was sick. She died five weeks ago.

Before I could hang up she said, "Wait a  minute. Are you Paul?"

"Yes" I said.

Well, Sally left a messsge for you.  I wrote it down in case you called. Let me read it to you." The note said, **"Tell him I still say there are other worlds to sing in. He'll know what I mean."

I thanked her and hung up the phone. I knew what Sally meant.

Never underestimate the impression you make on others. Whose life have you touched today."

# BREAD

November 2008

I remember , when I was a little boy, my Dad, on his way to work on a Saturday morning, would take my brother and me to visit our German grandparents in Portland. My dad owned a meat market named Yost Brothers Market in Portland, Oregon.

Grandma Yost

Saturday was my grandma's bake day. She began in the morning making German bread, apple turnovers, cabbage turnovers, noodles, and the loaves of bread had German strudel on top of it.

On Saturday evening, when my dad would come to pick us up to take us back home, she served supper for us to eat. She fried up German sausage cut up in circle pieces, provided bowls for the chicken soup with noodles she had made, and cut the bread into wide slices. Then we would spread a large coating of butter on each side of the bread. Boy, did I love the bread with the strudel on top with the German sausage, and the soup.

Recently I have been  learning to bake bread (no bread machine). My latest endeavor was making cinnamon rolls and were they good! The one problem I have faced is that I cannot create the strudel topping on my loaves of bread like Grandma put on top of her bread. That is my latest goal in my baking—to find out how to create that strudel.

Our Lord has much to do with providing bread. We read that He provided bread every morning called Manna for the nation of Israel to eat as they journeyed in the wilderness after they left Egypt. When Jesus gave the disciples a model prayer to pray, he taught them to ask for bread in the phrase *give us this day our daily bread.* (Matthew 6:11

After our Lord had spoken to a large crowd, they needed to eat before they traveled back home because they were located in a remote place. Jesus said to the disciples *"give them something to eat."* They replied that they had only five loaves of bread and two fish, and even eight months' wages would not buy enough bread for each one to have a bite. This was because there were about 5,000 men there, plus women and children. (Luke 9:13; John 6:7)

The account in Scripture states that Jesus took those five loaves and two fish, prayed, giving thanks to the Heavenly Father, then broke the bread and fish in pieces and told the disciples to pass out the food.  Each person there ate and was satisfied. When the disciples picked up what was left over, there were the twelve baskets full of broken pieces of fish and bread.

After feeding the 5,000, Jesus told the disciples to get in their boat and travel to the other side of the Sea of Galilee while He would dismiss the crowd.

While the disciples were travelling in the boat at 3 a.m. in the morning, a storm came up, and that is when Jesus walked on the water and they thought they were seeing a ghost.  The Bible records Him getting into the boat with them and the storm ceased and they arrived on  shore safe.

Jesus used these two experiences using bread to teach spiritual truths.

First of all, the scripture records the following: *then he climbed into the boat with them, and the wind died down. They were completely amazed for they had not understood about the loaves; their hearts were hardened.* The lesson was: if Christ could provide bread for more than 5,000 people, He could provide and protect the disciples when they faced a crisis.

Secondly, the crowd met Jesus and his disciples the next day after looking for them. Jesus again spoke to them saying, . *[25]And when they had found him on the other side of the sea, they said unto him, Rabbi, when camest thou hither? [26]Jesus answered them and Jesus said: I tell you the truth, you are looking for me, not because you saw miraculous signs but because you ate the loaves and had your fill. Do not work for food that spoils, but for food that endures to eternal life, which the Son of Man will give you. On him God the Father has placed his seal of approval .*"(John 6;25-27)

By using this example of bread which is found on the table of the. rich and poor, king and peasant, he taught those that were there a valuable truth about himself.

If a person follows him and invites him into his life, He provides spiritual life just as earthly bread provides physical life. The life He provides is: everlasting life (27, 47-51); satisfying life (35) as the multitude was satisfied and filled by the food he had multiplied, indwelling life (48-59), because as bread enters the body and becomes part of it, Christ enters the believer and becomes part of his life. He also provides resurrection life (37-47) because someday we will have a new resurrection body like His.

When grandma put the bread on the table, we could look at the bread, smell the bread, but it took action on our part to reach out and get a slice of that bread. The same holds true with Christ. We can know about Christ but we have to personally reach out and invite Him into our life.

This Thanksgiving, let it be a time of thanking Jesus Christ for coming as the Bread of Life who meets all the needs in our physical and spiritual life.

Here is a great illustration of how sin enslaves and forgiveness frees.

## A WISE GRANDMOTHER

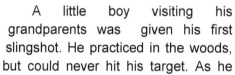 

A little boy visiting his grandparents was given his first slingshot. He practiced in the woods, but could never hit his target. As he came back to Grandma's back yard, he spied her pet duck. On impulse, he took aim, let the stone fly, and the duck fell dead. The boy panicked. Desperately afraid of the consequences, he hid the dead duck in the woodpile only to look up and see his sister, Sally, had seen it all.

After lunch that day, Grandma said, "Sally, let's wash the dishes." But Sally answered facetiously, "Johnny told me he wanted to help in the kitchen today. Didn't you, Johnny?" And she whispered to him, *"Remember the duck!"* So Johnny did the dishes.

Later Grandpa asked if the children wanted to go fishing. Grandma said, "I'm sorry, but I need Sally to help make supper." Sally smiled and said, "That's all arranged—Johnny wants to do it." Again she whispered, *"Remember the duck."* Johnny stayed while Sally went fishing. After several days of Johnny's doing both *his* and *Sally's* chores, he finally could stand it no longer. He confessed to Grandma that he had killed her duck.

"I know, Johnny," Grandma said, giving him a hug. "I was standing at the window and saw the whole thing. Because I love you, I forgave you, but I wondered how long you would let Sally use this incident to make a slave of you."

*Pulpit Help* ,,published by AMG Publishers, Chattanooga, TN 37421

# GOD'S PRESENCE
# THE SHEKINAH GLORY

October 2009

Have you ever looked into the sky and thought that one of the clouds that you are looking at just might be the cloud that the Lord Jesus Christ is going to come out of when he calls believers up to Him to take them to heaven?

When Jesus left the earth to go back to heaven, he ascended up into a cloud. Two men who appeared clad in white said, "Men of Galilee, why do you stand here looking into the sky? This same Jesus, Who has been taken from you into heaven will come back in the same way you have seen Him go into heaven." (Acts 1:11 NIV)

The Holy Spirit dwells in that cloud.

This cloud is mentioned several times in the Old and New Testament and is called the *Shekinah Glory*. The actual word *Shekinah* does not appear in the Bible, but *Shacan,* the root from which it comes, does appear. It means *to dwell.* Combining the word with God's glory, *Shekinah Glory* has come to stand for *a visible manifestation of God's presence among men.*

The *Shekinah Glory* is seen in various forms. The most common are light, fire, a cloud, or a combination of these, and sometimes the voice of God comes forth from it.

This month I have a challenge for you. I will be referring to some examples of its appearance in the Bible, but will also give some scriptures so you can follow up in your own personal Bible study. A blessing is in store for you as you will see how God revealed Himself to men and women.

Some examples of the *Shekinah Glory* being present in the Old Testament are:

Moses saw it manifested by fire through the burning bush. (Exodus 3:6) Moses recognized God's presence in the bush and took off his shoes because the ground was holy, and God spoke to him out of the fire.

It appeared when God led Israel across the wilderness. Exodus 13:21, 22; Numbers 9:17-22 God went before them, and led them in a pillar of a cloud by day and a pillar of fire by night.

The cloud protected Israel at the Red Sea by darkness and light. ( Exodus 14:19- 24)

It appeared when Israel murmured in the Zin wilderness. (Ex. 16:7-10)

It appeared when God spoke to Moses on Mt. Sinai and God gave him the Ten Commandments. Moses was on the mountain for 40 days and 40 nights. overshadowed by the cloud. (Ex. 24:15-18) It is interesting to note that Moses received a vision of the Lord in that cloud, and the result was that his face shined when he came back down off the mountain. ( Exodus 34:5-7, 29-35)

*The Shekinah Glory* filled both the Tabernacle and Solomon's Temple when they were dedicated. (Exodus. 40:34-38; 1 Kings 8:10, 11; 2 Chron. 5:13, 14)

It stood above the mercy seat in the Holy of Holies in the Tabernacle. (Leviticus 16:2 with Ex. 25:22; Cf. Hebrews 9:5)

For further study in the Old Testament, consult Exodus 9:9-25; Numbers 11:16-25; 12:1; 14:14; 16:42; Ezekiel 9:3; 10:4; 10:18.

Some examples in the New Testament when the *Shekinah Glory* was present are:.

It appeared to the shepherds at Christ's birth (Luke 2:8, 9 Cf. John 1:14)

It was present at Christ's baptism. *16And Jesus, when he was baptized, went up straightway out of the water: and, lo, the heavens were opened unto him, and he saw the Spirit of God descending like a dove, and lighting upon him: 17And lo a voice from heaven, saying, This is my beloved Son, in whom I am well pleased.* (Matthew 3:16, 17)

It was present at Christ's Transfiguration. *1And after six days Jesus taketh Peter, James, and John his brother, and bringeth them up into an high mountain apart, 2And was transfigured before them: and his face did shine as the sun, and his raiment was white as the light. 3And, behold, there appeared unto them Moses and Elias talking with him. 4Then answered Peter, and said unto Jesus, Lord, it is good for us to be here: if thou wilt, let us make here three tabernacles; one for thee, and one for Moses, and one for Elias. 5While he yet spake, behold, a bright cloud overshadowed them: and behold a voice out of the cloud, which said, This is my beloved Son, in whom I am well pleased; hear ye him. 6And when the disciples heard it, they fell on their face, and were sore afraid. 7And Jesus came and touched them, and said, Arise, and be not afraid. 8And when they had lifted up their eyes, they saw no man, save Jesus only.* (Matthew 17:1-8)

It was present at Christ's ascension (Acts 1:9) and will be present when He calls up believers to heaven at the rapture. (1 Thessalonians. 4:13-18)

It will appear during the tribulation, the time of God's judgment of those on earth, at the funeral of God's two witnesses (Revelation 11:12)

It will appear at the second coming of Christ to the earth after the tribulation. (Dan. 7:13,14; Ezek. 43:1-5; Matt. 24:30, 64; Rev. 1:7; 14:14)

**Where is the *Shekinah Glory* today?**

73

In 2 Corinthians 3:18 Paul gave a dissertation and in verse 18 he writes: *And we, who with unveiled faces all reflect the Lord's glory, are being transformed into his likeness with ever-increasing glory which comes from the Lord, who is the Spirit.* He continues in 4:6, *For God, who said, "Let light shine out of darkness," make his light shine in our hearts to give us the light of the knowledge of God's glory displayed in the face of Christ.* 2 Corinthians 4:6 .*NIV*

Are you ready for a profound truth? If you are a believer, Paul is saying that God the Holy Spirit who dwells in the believer, produces a reflection of God's glory (the *Shekinah Glory*) that can be seen on the face of a believer just like Moses experienced when he came off of the mountain after being in the presence of the Lord when he received the Ten Commandments.

Have you seen believers that "glowed" reflecting God's Glory on their face? I have. I had a teacher at Multnomah School of the Bible whose face was radiant.

I have seen other believers who have a deep walk with the Lord who radiate a glow of the Lord. It can come by reading God's Word, spending time in prayer with the Lord, or in some cases a person is so close to the Lord he or she manifests a heavenly radiance of God's presence in their life.

A VISIBLE MANIFESTATION OF GOD'S PRESENCE

**GOD'S SHEKINAH GLORY**

A CLOUD FIRE LIGHT HIS VOICE A COMBINATION

Illustration 2.

# WHAT ILLNESS HAS TAUGHT ME"

January 2006

*The following article has been taken from The Log of the Good Ship Grace, Haven of Rest Ministries, Vol. 31; No. 32, 1965, by First Mate Bob.*

It was my privilege to know personally Martha Snell Nicholson, that dear saint of God who wrote hundreds of beautiful and cheerful Christian poems although her body was literally wracked by pain.

I recently came across an article that Mrs. Nicholson wrote, titled, "What Illness Has Taught Me".

I share it with you, especially you shut-ins, in the hope that it will make your lamp of faith burn brighter during your dark days of suffering.

Listen carefully to these touching words from the pen of the late Martha Snell Nicholson

Looking back over nearly a lifetime of illness, I am thanking God for these pain-filled years. When I stood at the beginning and strained my eyes to see down the dim path ahead, I was sure it would be strewed with roses. When pain and sorrow came I could not understand, but now as I look back the long road which lies so clearly behind me, I see that His hand was upon me all the way.

"Never strong as a child, I broke down very early in young womanhood. I spent the ensuing seven years in bed most of the time with T.B., then up off and on, one sick spell fter another, seven operations, besides fifteen minor carvings. It seems that almost every  disease has had a try at me. For the last twenty years I have been on the shelf, unable to attend church only once during that time.

"They have brought me gifts—those weary years. I do not enjoy sickness or suffering, or the nervous agony and exhaustion that are harder to bear than physical pain. And an invalid must bury so many dear dreams which have death struggles and refuse to die decently and quietly. But God has a way of taking away our toys, and after we have cried for a while like disappointed children, He fills our hands with jewels, which cannot be valued with the gold of Ophir, and the precious onyx, or the sapphire.

"It seems odd that I can thank Him for sleeplessness. I have suffered so from it, and yet, looking back, I can see that some of the greatest blessings have come during the long nights. At about two in the morning, when all the world .is quiet, God comes very close. Sometimes when I have been wakeful for hours with fever or pain, or have tossed bout, restlessly trying to solve the problems, financial and domestic, that come when someone in the home is ill, at last the thought has come, 'How foolish of me. I don't have to attend to this; He will do it for me.'" And have whispered over and over to myself some of His precious promises, and they were indeed a lamp unto my feet in the night.

"Of course one of the hardest things about being sick is a feeling of uselessness. We want to work for God. Can it be that we have an idea that God is needy, that our services are necessary to Him? Oh, it is indeed good to work for God, but it is better just to do His will, and it may be that it is not His will that all should work. Some day He will tell us about that.

"But there is one great ministry in which even we sick ones may share, and I thank God for that—the ministry of prayer. It is a marvelous, a breath-taking thought, that I, lying here on my bed in my small room, may help set in operation the vast machinery of God, may change the destiny of a life, a world, may even hasten the day of His appearing! Why don't we pray more?

"I recall that after I had been sick for several years, I thought, in my foolishness, that I had learned still sick. I do not understand why I must still be an invalid. I no longer expect to understand. If I did, there would be no need of faith. Enough that He knows why and some day He will tell me all about it—why it was best for me and best for His cause.

"But the best part of all is the blessed hope of His soon coming. How I ever lived before I grasped that wonderful truth, I do not know. How anyone lives without it these trying days. I cannot imagine. Each morning I think, with a leap of the heart 'he may come today!' and each evening, 'When I awake, I may be in glory!' Each day must be lived as though it were to be my last, and there is so much to be done, to purify myself and to set my house in order.

"I am on tiptoe with expectance. There are no more grey days for they are all touched with color—no more dark days, for the radiance of His coming is on the horizon—no more dull days, with glory just around the corner—and no more lonely days, with His footsteps coming ever nearer, and the thought that soon I shall see His blessed face, and be forever through with pain and tears!"

Haven Ministries  server@haventoday.org.

'

'

## WHEN I SAY ... "I am a Christian"

When I say... "I am a Christian,
I'm not shouting "I'm clean livin'."
I'm whispering "I was lost,
Now I'm found and forgiven."

When I say... "I am a Christian"
I don't speak of this with pride.
I'm confessing that I stumble
And need Christ to be my guide.

When I say... "I am a Christian"
I'm not trying to be strong.
I'm professing that I'm weak
And need His strength to carry on.

When I say... "I am a Christian"
I'm not bragging of success.
I'm admitting I have failed
And need God to clean my mess.

When I say... "I am a Christian"
I'm not claiming to be perfect.
My flaws are far too visible
But God believes I am worth it.

When I say... "I am a Christian"
I still feel the sting of pain.
I have my share of heartaches
So I call upon His name.

When I say... "I am a Christian"
I'm not holier than thou.'
I'm just a simple sinner
Who received God's good grace, somehow.
                              -Maya Angelou

# A FRUIT BEARER

October 2004

*I came across the following true story that I want to share with you this month in .he publication Pulpit Helps by Wayne Norton. He writes:*

Several years ago, Dr. John Claypool was the senior pastor of Broadway Baptist Church in Fort Worth, Texas. He was very much in demand as a speaker. Dr. Claypool came to a train terminal to catch a waiting train for a speaking engagement.

Ahead of Dr. Claypool was a hurried businessman who was navigating through the crowd like a football player. The man was just ahead of Dr. Claypool when he rounded a corner. A disabled little boy had a table with candy, gum, and other snacks. The businessman knocked the little boy down and his table to the terminal floor. The table spilled merchandise everywhere. The businessman looked at the crying little merchant and cursed him for being in the way.

Dr. Claypool stopped, picked up the chair, sat the little boy in it, handed him a handkerchief, and began to retrieve all the scattered merchandise and money. After the boy was "back in business," Dr. Claypool handed him a twenty dollar bill. The little boy stopped crying and said, **"Mister, are you Jesus Christ?"** Dr. Claypool smiled and replied, "No son, I'm not. I am just trying to do the things that He would do if He were here." (Wayne Norton quoted by *Pulpit Helps*, , published by AMG Publishers, Chattanooga, TN 37422)

When Jesus was baptized by John the baptizer, the Holy Spirit came down and indwelled Jesus Christ in His humanity. (Luke 3:21; 4:1) Jesus did His ministry through the power of the Holy Spirit (Isaiah 11:1-5.) ."

Every person who has invited Jesus Christ into their

life as Lord and Savior has Jesus Christ living in them through the indwelling ministry of the Holy Spirit. (1 Corinthians 6:19) As a result our lives should evidence the same type of life Jesus lived as Paul writes in Colossians 1:27 *"Christ in you, the hope of glory.* See also Galatians 2:20

In the book of Galatians that kind of life is likened to fruit produced by the Holy Spirit in a believer's life (Galatians 5:22, 23) to reflect Jesus Christ in our lives . The fruit of the Spirit is LOVE and the following words give the qualities or flavors of love; joy, peace, patience, kindness, goodness, faithfulness, gentleness and self-control.

Briefly, how were these qualities of love evidenced in the life of Jesus Christ?

**Love:** When Jesus saw the rich young man who came to Him it says, "Jesus looked at him and loved him (Mark 10:21) and of course His love was shown when He died on the cross for us. (Romans 5:8; John 3:16)

Joy: Jesus prayed to the Father these words: "I am coming to you now, but I say these things while I am still in the world, so that they may have the full measure of my joy within them." John 17:13; also John 15:11

**Peace**: He spoke of leaving His peace with the disciples at the Last Supper. "Peace I leave with you, my peace I give you. I do not give to you as the world gives. Do not let your hearts be troubled and do not be afraid."
(John 14:27)

**Patience**: [Greek word meaning stead-fastness under provocation, patiently enduring ill-treatment without anger or thought of retaliation or revenge]. Think of Jesus on the cross saying,("Father forgive them for

80

they know not what they are doing." (Luke 23:34; 2 Peter 2:21-24)

**Kindness or gentleness**: Small children sensed His gentleness and He showed this when He said: "Let the little children come to me, and do not hinder them, for the kingdom of heaven belongs to such as these." Matthew 19:14

**Goodness**: [Greek word speaks of the highest moral and ethical values] When Jesus cleansed the temple He was showing goodness because they had desecrated the place of worship making it a bazaar.

**Faithfulness**: [conveys the idea of trustworthiness and strict observance of promises] In prayer we see Jesus showing this when He prayed: "I have brought you glory on earth by completintleness: [Another word used to define this is meekness which is power, strength, spirit, and wildness under control.] Isaiah describes Jesus before the cross: "He was oppressed and He was afflicted, yet He did like a sheep that is silent before its shearers, so He did not open His mouth; Like a lamb that is led to slaughter, and did not open His mouth." Isaiah. 53:7

**Self-Control**: speaking of mastery, able to control one's thoughts and actions. When confronted by questions by the religious leaders to trip Him up, Jesus showed self control when He answered them back. Luke 20:19-47

Wayne Norton sums it up by writing: " If we are a follower of Christ, then we too can be doing what Jesus would do and being what Jesus would be if He were in our shoes." ibid

# THE FRUIT
# OF
# THE HOLY SPIRIT

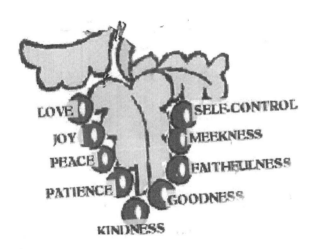

ILLUSTRATION 3

# HE BECAME ONE OF US

September 2002

Sometimes when a Christian reads the Scriptures they convey thoughts that absolutely overwhelm their understanding. That happened to me recently when I was reading in the book of *Hebrews* during my devotions. The book of Hebrews is a very deep book and the writer conveys deep truths about God throughout the book. I came across one of those teachings that really got me thinking.

Here are the verses that challenged my mind and heart:

7Who in the days of his flesh, when he had offered up prayers and supplications with strong crying and tears unto him that was able to save him from death, and was heard in that he feared; 8Though he were a Son, yet learned he obedience by the things which he suffered; 9And being made perfect, he became the author of eternal salvation unto all them that obey him;

(Hebrews 5:7-9 NIV)

These verses speak of the humanity of Jesus Christ. Jesus Christ was and is the Second Person of the Trinity. He is God the Son, as the verses note, but He became human, *"became one of us"* (Hebrews 2:14) , so that he might die for you and for me as the perfect sacrifice for our sins.

I began to really ponder the fact that he became one of us and suffered before he could learn what it really means to obey God.

Jesus became like you and me.

Physically, **He had a body of flesh** like us. He experienced all that we face in life as we grow up. .His mother had to change his diapers as a baby. (Luke 2:40).

He learned the trade of carpentry as a boy from his father. (Matthew 13:55; Mark 6:3). He experienced being so tired that he had to get some sleep because he had spent the whole day teaching the crowd (Mark 14:24). He had an appetite for food (Matt. 42; 21:18) he got thirsty (John 4:7; 19:28). We suffer physical pain, but think of the physical pain he suffered when nails were put through his hands and his feet let alone the severe pain he suffered as a man when they beat him and put a crown of thorns on his head. He was so weak from the loss of blood that they got a man to help him carry his cross on the way to Golgotha (Mark 15:15-21).

**Jesus also had a soul** like you and me do and experienced sorrow and shed tears at the grave of Lazarus. (John 11:35)   John shares that his soul was troubled (John 12:27) He was dependent on his Father for strength through prayer. (Mark 1:35; John 6:15; Heb. 5:7)

Having a soul he felt genuine love and shared love to others when he saw the crowds were like sheep without a shepherd. (Matt. 9:36; Mark 6:34).

When he was in the upper room before he went to the cross it's stated "having loved his own who were in the world", he now showed them the full extent of his love" (John 13:1b) just to name a few references about his love. Robert Schuller shares that Jesus experienced a *sixth wound,* a deep wound emotionally when Judas betrayed him and kissed him on the cheek (Matt. 26:49). (*Healing for the Hidden Wound,* 1984).

**He had a spirit** like you and me. Examples given in the Word of God are: "Jesus perceiving in his spirit" (Mark 2:8), "and he sighed deeply in his spirit" (Mark 8:12), "Father into your hands I commend my spirit" (Luke 23:46), and "he was troubled in the spirit" (John 13:21). Through his spirit he communicated with the Father in prayer throughout his time on earth, especially in the garden. (Luke 22:39-44).

We are people of flesh and blood. That is why Jesus became one of us. He died to destroy the devil, who had given power of death.(.Job 1:13-19) But he also died to rescue all of us who live each day in fear of dying. Jesus clearly did not come to help angels, but he did come to help Abraham's descendants (that's you and me too). He had to be one of us, so that he could sacrifice himself for the forgiveness of our sins and then serve God as our merciful and faithful high priest. And now that Jesus has suffered and was tempted, he can help anyone else who is tempted. Heb. 2:14-18

Jesus is the eternal Son of God who is Lord of Lords and King of Kings. One Who is our Creator (John 1:3; Colossians 1:15-18; John 1:1; Hebrews 1:1-3). But we need to be reminded he became human like you and me and faced all the difficulties we face today and he cares about you and me as our Lord and Savior. He cares about all that we are experiencing in our life. THANK YOU JESUS

BIBLE VERSES: HEBREWS 5:7-10

[5]So also Christ glorified not himself to be made an high priest; but he that said unto him, Thou art my Son, to day have I begotten thee. [6]As he saith also in another *place*, Thou *art* a priest for ever after the order of Melchisedec. [7]Who in the days of his flesh, when he had offered up prayers and supplications with strong crying and tears unto him that was able to save him from death, and was heard in that he feared; [8]Though he were a Son, yet learned he

obedience by the things which he suffered; [9]And being made perfect, he became the author of eternal salvation unto all them that obey him

# CONSIDER

•Have you ever been pricked by a rose thorn? IT HURT, DIDN'T IT? Consider that it was not one thorn, but a crown of thorns, which was pressed down—hard—upon our dear Savior's head.

•Have you ever tried dragging a large wooden beam any distance? The other day I tried moving the piano by myself. It wasn't easy.

•Have you been humiliated lately? I mean, really embarrassed...The shame, the embarrassment of a humiliating experience is dreadful.

•Have you ever stepped on a nail? I remember very well the time I did. It was awfully painful. Consider the excruciating pain of being nailed to a cross—a splintery cross. The searing pain.

•Consider the agony as the cross was roughly hoisted into the air and then dropped with a hard, hard thud into a hole prepared for it. The flesh ripping...

•These aren't pretty pictures. Crucifixion wasn't a pretty thing! Nor was it fashionable!

•We have the "good news" of the resurrection to share, but the experience of the crucifixion was Christ's alone to bear.

•This is what Jesus did for what today is called "Easter."                    Author Unknown, *The Exchange*

# JESUS CHRIST
# OUR HIGH PRIEST
November 2009

The book of Hebrews records these words in chapter 4:

*12For the word of God is quick, and powerful, and sharper than any twoedged sword, piercing even to the dividing asunder of soul and spirit, and of the joints and marrow, and is a discerner of the thoughts and intents of the heart. 13Neither is there any creature that is not manifest in his sight: but all things are naked and opened unto the eyes of him with whom we have to do. 14Seeing then that we have a great high priest, that is passed into the heavens, Jesus the Son of God, let us hold fast our profession. 15For we have not an high priest which cannot be touched with the feeling of our infirmities; but was in all points tempted like as we are, yet without sin. 16Let us therefore come boldly unto the throne of grace, that we may obtain mercy, and find grace to help in time of need.* Hebrews 4:12-16)

This is the time of the year that is set aside for us to stop in the mad rush of our lives and set aside a time to be thankful, and what better thing there is  to do than to express our thankfulness to our Savior for praying for us.

In the Old Testament, the people of Israel came in touch with God through their high priest, who offered sacrifices for their daily sins.  Once a year the high priest, on the Day of Atonement, would enter the Holy of Holies in the Temple to offer the sacrifice ordained by God to cover the sin of the people.  A curtain separated the Holy Place in the Temple from the Holy of Holies. It was so serious that a rope was tied to the High Priest in case he made an error in presenting the sacrifice to God and they had to pull him out of the Holy of Holies because he hadn't followed God's instructions perfectly in offering the sacrifice and was struck dead..

When Jesus died on the cross, something happened that revolutionized a personal relationship to God, because Jesus Christ offered the perfect sacrifice by shedding His blood for all sinful mankind. God indicated that our Lord's sacrifice was sufficient when the curtain tore from top to bottom between the Holy Place and the Holy of Holies.(Matt. 27:51) "The tearing of that curtain, which was a type of the human body of Christ (Heb. 10:20) signified that a "new and living way" was opened for all believers into the very presence of God, with no other sacrifice or priesthood except Christ's. (Heb. 9:1-8; 10:19-22)

The Apostle Paul wrote in the book of Romans, *34Who is he that condemneth? It is Christ that died, yea rather, that is risen again, who is even at the right hand of God, who also maketh intercession for us.*(Romans 8:34)

I don't know about you, but I am so very thankful that Jesus prays for me because I sure need it.

An example of Jesus praying for us is when He told Peter: during the Last Supper, that He had prayed for him because He knew Peter was going to deny knowing Him: "*And the Lord said, Simon, Simon, behold, Satan hath desired to have you, that he may sift you as wheat: 32But I have prayed for thee, that thy faith fail not: and when thou art converted, strengthen thy brethren.*

*33And he said unto him, Lord, I am ready to go with thee, both into prison, and to death.*

*34And he said, I tell thee, Peter, the cock shall not crow this day, before that thou shalt thrice deny that thou knowest me.* (Luke 22:31-34, 32)

And we all know what happened. Peter denied the Lord three times. He desperately needed the prayers of Christ for him.

It is encouraging to read the prayer that Jesus offered the night He was taken captive as recorded in John 17, when He prayed for His disciples and included all believers who would come after his work on the cross.

Note verse 20 as He prays, *20Neither pray I for these alone but for them also which shall believe on me through their word"*

The Apostle John wrote. *1My little children, these things write I unto you, that ye sin not. And if any man sin, we have an advocate with the Father, Jesus Christ the righteous: 2And he is the propitiation for our sins: and not for ours only, but also for the sins of the whole world. (1 John 2:1,2)*

This brings me back to Hebrews 4, where it shows us that Christ understands our weakness because He was also tempted and tested in the areas we are tested in, but He didn't sin. He's praying for us as we travel down this road of life. He knows our weaknesses just like He knew the weaknesses of Peter and the disciples.

If we know Christ as our Savior, we have Jesus who cares about us. He knows what's ahead of us just like He knew what was ahead for Peter and we have His prayers being offered on our behalf.

How thankful I am that Jesus is praying for me. Why don't you tell him that you are thankful too.

BIBLE VERSES: JOHN 17

# HEBREWS 4:14-16

[14]Seeing then
that we have a great high priest,
that is passed into the heavens,
Jesus the Son of God,
let us hold fast *our* profession.
[15]For we have not an high priest which
cannot be touched with the feeling of our
infirmities;
but was in all points tempted like as *we
are, yet* without sin.
[16]Let us therefore come boldly unto the
throne of grace,
that we may obtain mercy, and find grace
to help in time of need.

# THE LORD IS MY ROCK
September 2012

Vernon J. Charlesworth wrote the words and Ira S. Sankey wrote the music to a familiar hymn, *A Shelter In the Time of Storm.* based on the wonderful truth that the Lord calls Himself the **Rock** in the Scripture. The words are as follows:

> Lord's our Rock, in Him we hide,
> A shelter in the time of storm;
> Secure whatever ill betide,
> A shelter in the time of storm.
>
> A shade by day, defense by night,
> A shelter in the time of storm;
> No fears alarm, no foes affright,
> A shelter in the time of storm.
>
> The raging storms may round us beat
> A shelter in the time of storm:
> We'll never leave our safe retreat;
> A shelter in the time of storm.
>
> O Rock divine, O Refuge dear,
> A shelter in the time of storm,
> Be Thou our helper ever near,
> A shelter in the time of storm.
>
> Oh, Jesus is a Rock in a weary land,
> A weary land, a weary land;
> Oh Jesus is a Rock in a weary land,
> A shelter in the time of storm.

The Holy Spirit used the image of a rock in the Scriptures many times to show how God is the Rock in a believer's life.

91

THOUGHTS from REFLECTIONS

David testifies time and time again in the Psalms that God was his Rock. One example is in Psalm 18 when he wrote:

1. *I love you, O LORD , my **strength**. The LORD is my **rock**, my **fortress** and my **deliverer;** my God is my **rock,** in whom I take **refuge**, my **shield** and the **horn of my salvation**, my **stronghold**. For who is God besides the LORD? And who is the **Rock** except our God?...As for God, his way is perfect; the word of the LORD is flawless. He is a **shield** for all who make **refuge** in him. For who is God besides the LORD? And who is the **Rock** except our God? It is God who arms me with **strength** and makes my way perfect....The LORD lives! Praise be to my **Rock**! Exalted be God my Savior!* (Psalm 18:1-3, 30-32, 46)

The Hebrew word for "*rock*" that is used is "*sur*" which denotes a rocky wall, cliff, rocky hill, mountain. The Greek word "*petra*" is translated *"rock"* in the New Testament which denotes a "*massive rock*" and is distinct from "*petros*" meaning a stone that might be thrown or easily moved.

Using David's description of God being the Rock in his life in Psalm 18, I want to focus how God is a Rock in our lives as Christians.

First of all, He is **"my Rock "**. When Jesus was on earth He gave a parable about two houses that were built-- one whose foundation was built on sand and the other that was built on a rock. He said:

[24]"Therefore everyone who hears these words of mine and puts them into practice is like a wise man who built his n the rock. [25]The rain came down, the streams rose, and the winds blew and beat against that house; yet it did not fall, because it had its foundation on the rock. [26]But everyone who hears these words of mine and does not put them into

practice is like a foolish man who built his house on sand. ²⁷The rain came down, the streams rose, and the winds blew and beat against that house, and it fell with a great crash.( Matthew 7:24-27)

When we invite Christ into our lives, our feet are planted solidly on the Rock which is Jesus Christ, who is God the Son, and He becomes our Savior. *For no one can lay any foundation other than the one already laid, which is Jesus Christ.*(1 Corinthians. 3:11)

Having God as his Rock, David shares in Psalm 18 what the Lord provided as his Rock of salvation in his daily life, and it is true in our daily lives, too.

The Lord provides **strength** in our daily living. God as our Rock makes the difference between struggling and trusting. It is the difference between Christianity and religion because it is personal.

Paul wrote, .I can do all things through Christ, because He strengtheneth me. Philippians 4:13

God hasn't promised to remove the difficulties we face in our lives, but He has promised to infuse strength in us as we face the difficulties that confront us. When we feel weak, we can be assured that He will be there to give us strength.

The Lord is our **fortress.** Literally the Hebrew word used for fortress means "mountain castle". Here is the picture of a castle on top oTf the rock signifying God being the ruler and protecting that which is below. How aptly the poet who wrote:

"O safe to the Rock that is higher than I,
My soul in its conflicts and sorrows would fly.
So sinful, so weary, Thine, Thine, would I be:
Thou blest "Rock of Ages", I'm hiding in Thee.
Hiding in Thee, Hiding in Thee,
Thou blest "Rock of Ages," I'm hiding in Thee.

The Lord as our Rock is our **shield.** Paul wrote,
*Finally, be strong in the Lord and in his mighty power. Put on the full armor of God so that you can take your stand against*

*the devil's schemes For our struggle is not against flesh and blood, but against the ruler, against the authorities, against the powers of this dark world and against the spiritual forces of evil in the heavenly realms. Therefore put on the full armor of God, so that when the day of evil comes, you may be able to stand your ground, and after you have done everything, to stand.*(Ephesians 6:10-13) Having God as our Rock gives us that protection when we are being attacked spiritually.

The Lord as our  Rock is our **refuge.** There are many kinds of storms that confront us.  I heard of a painting of a small bird that is being protected by a cleft in a rock as a storm is taking place. The hymn that I quoted at the beginning shares how God is truly our shelter in the time of storm.

The Lord is the **horne of our salvation.** The word "horn" in the Hebrew means "peak".  As a mountain has a peak so God as our Rock is the peak of our salvation. All spiritual and physical blessings culminate in Him.

Is your heart filled with praise and love for the Lord like David because the LORD is your ROCK? David expressed it by writing  this psalm of praise beginning with the words "I love you, O LORD, my strength."

*Come, let us sing for joy to the LORD: Let us shout aloud to the Rock of our salvation. Let us come before him with thanksgiving and extol him with music and song.* **Psalm 95:2)**

# OUR LOVING HEAVENLY FATHER
August , September 2004

[I wrote two articles about our Heavenly Father in 2004, and have saved and edited them because of length.]

Many of us enjoyed the television series *Touched by an Angel.* Even though Jesus Christ was seldom mentioned, the series accomplished the goal of making people aware of the existence of a Heavenly Father who was personally interested in them.

I have written in Reflections about the ministry of Jesus Christ, and the Holy Spirit. Recently I have felt the desire to find out more about the first person of the Trinity, God the Father.

The night before Jesus was crucified, Philip in the Upper Room requested, "Lord,show us the Father."

*Jesus answered:"Don't you know me Philip, even after I have been among you such a long time? Anyone who has seen me has seen the Father. How can you say, 'show us the Father'? Don't you believe that I am in the Father, and that the Father is in me.? The words I say to you I do not speak on my own authority. Rather it is the Father, living in me, who is doing His work."* John 14:8-10 NIV

Jesus states that same night in His prayer to the Father that He was sent to reveal the Father *"Righteous Father, though the world does not know you, I know you, and they know that you have sent me. 26 I have made you known to them, and will continue to make you known in order that the love you have for me may be in them and that I myself may be in them."* (John 17:25, 26 NIV)

God the Father made a plan before the world was created, knowing man would sin and separate himself from the Holy Trinity, to send His Son to become the sacrifice for

95

man so that the relationship might be established again with the Father. That plan is recorded in the book of Ephesians 1:4-14.

If a person believes in Jesus Christ as their Savior, and invites Him into their life, a relationship is established and God becomes their Heavenly Father for eternity. For God so loved the world that He gave His one and only Son that whoever believes in Him will not perish but have everlasting life. John 3:16 NIV

I want to spend the rest of this article thinking about our wonderful Heavenly Father and the privileges we have as His child.

First of all, He loves us very much. God is love.(1 John 4:9) In fact, He loves us the same way He loves our Lord Jesus Christ, which is an awesome thought (John 17:23), and showers His love upon us in many, any ways. Let us list some of them.

1. We will never be separated from His love. "For "I am convinced that neither death nor life, neither angels nor demons, neither the present nor the future, nor any powers, neither height nor depth, nor anything else in all creation, will be able to separate us from the love of God that is in Christ Jesus our Lord." (Romans 8:38, 39).

2. He wants us to address Him as Father (Abba, Daddy). It's the same word used by Jesus in the Garden. (Romans 8:15; Galatians 4:6; Mark 14:38). We can come to Him anytime, anywhere, and He listens to us when we talk to Him in prayer. He is Spirit (John 4:23, 24) so we communicate with Him with our spirit.

3. He will supply all of our needs "So do not worry, saying, 'What shall we eat? Or 'What shall we drink?' or 'What hall we wear?' ...your heavenly Father knows that you

need them." (Matthew 6:11, 12; James 1:16; Philippians 4:19)

4. He is with us continually *⁵Let your* conduct *be* without covetousness; *be* content with such things as you have. For He Himself has said, *"I will never leave you nor forsake you."* ⁶So we may boldly say:
*"The LORD is my helper;*
*I will not fear.*
*What can man do to me?"* NKJV

"You have made known to me the path of life; you will fill me with joy in your presence with eternal pleasures at your right hand." (Psalm 16:11 NKJV; Psalm 139)

5. He disciplines and teaches us as a loving Father so that we will become partakers of His holiness to make us like Jesus. (Proverbs 3:12; Hebrews 12:9-11)

6. He expresses praise and appreciation and rewards those who earnestly seek and honor Him (Job 1; Hebrews 11:6)

7. He creates joy when we are with Him. (Psalm 16:11

8. He protects us from our enemy the devil. (John 17:15; Matthew 6:13)

9. He has prepared a special home for us where we will spend the future with Him. (John 14:1-5)

# OUR RELATIONSHIP WITH THE FATHER
# HAS BEEN ESTABLISHED

When Mary Magdalene met Jesus in the garden after Jesus rose from the grave  Jesus Christ announced what had been accomplished:

[11]But Mary stood without at the sepulchre weeping: and as she wept, she stooped down, *and looked* into the sepulchre, [12]And seeth two angels in white sitting, the one at the head, and the other at the feet, where the body of Jesus had lain. [13]And they say unto her, Woman, why weepest thou? She saith unto them, Because they have taken away my Lord, and I know not where they have laid him. [14]And when she had thus said, she turned herself back, and saw Jesus standing, and knew not that it was esus. [1]

[5]Jesus saith unto her, Woman, why weepest thou? whom seekest thou?

She, supposing him to be the gardener, saith unto him, Sir, if thou have borne him hence, tell me where thou hast laid him, and I will take him away.

[16]Jesus saith unto her, Mary.

She turned herself, and saith unto him, Rabboni; which is to say, Master.

[17]Jesus saith unto her, Touch me not; for I am not yet ascended to my Father: but go to my brethren, and say unto them, I ascend unto my Father, and your Father; and *to* my God, and your God.

Note the new relationship with the Father and God had been accomplished! **My Father and Your Father, My God and Your God!**  John 20:1-17

# GIVING THANKS
# FOR GOD'S PROTECTION
November 2007

This month is a month that we have set aside to give God our thanks for His many blessings He bestows on us **who trust in Him.**

I've been reflecting on the fact that He protects us and has given illustrations in His Word of Him doing it to encourage those who trust in Him.

Psalm 34:7 tells us the Lord Himself watches over us. *"The angel of the LORD encamps around those who fear him, and he delivers them."* (The phrase *"angel of the LORD"* is used again and again to speak of the LORD Himself in the Old Testament).

Jesus spoke of the Heavenly Father's care for His children when He said, ""Behold the fowls of the air: for they sow not, neither do they reap, nor gather into barns; yet your heavenly Father feedeth them. Are ye not much better than they? (Matthew 6:26, 27  see also 10:29)

God protects his children by providing guardian angels to watch over and protect us. In Hebrews 1:14 we read, *"Are not all angels ministering spirits sent to serve those who will inherit eternal life?"* NIV"

David wrote under the guidance of God, *"Whoever dwells in the shelter of the Most High will rest in the shadow of the Almighty. I will say of the LORD, 'He is my refuge and my fortress, my God, in whom I trust."'..."For he will command his angels concerning you to guard you in all your ways; they will lift you up in their hands,so that you will not strike your foot against a stone '(Psalm 91:1,2,11,12 NIV])*

God sent a band of angels to protect Elisha the prophet from Aram the king . We read what took place.

*14Therefore sent he thither horses, and chariots, and a great host: and they came by night, and compassed the city about. 15And when the servant of the man of God was risen early, and gone forth, behold, an host compassed the city both with horses and chariots.*

*And his servant said unto him, Alas, my master! how shall we do?*

*16And he answered, Fear not: for they that be with us are more than they that be with them. 17And Elisha prayed, and said, LORD, I pray thee, open his eyes, that he may see. And the LORD opened the eyes of the young man; and he saw: and, behold, the mountain was full of horses and chariots of fire round about Elisha.*

*18And when they came down to him, Elisha prayed unto the LORD, and said, Smite this people, I pray thee, with blindness. And he smote them with blindness according to the word of Elisha.*

*19And Elisha said unto them, This is not the way, neither is this the city: follow me, and I will bring you to the man whom ye seek. But he led them to Samaria. 20And it came to pass, when they were come into Samaria, that Elisha said, LORD, open the eyes of these men, that they may see. And the LORD opened their eyes, and they saw; and, behold, they were in the midst of Samaria. 21And the king of Israel said unto Elisha, when he saw them, My father, shall I smite them? shall I smite them? 22And he answered, Thou shalt not smite them: wouldest thou smite those whom thou hast taken captive with thy sword and with thy bow? set bread and water before them, that they may eat and drink, and go to their master. 23And he prepared great provision for them: and when they had eaten and drunk, he sent them away, and they went to their master. So the bands of Syria came no more into the land of Israel. 2 Kings 6:14-23*

All those who know their Bible know how God protected Shadrach, Meshach and Abednego when they were cast into the flames of the blazing furnace. The prophet Daniel was also protected from being the meal of the lions when he was cast into the lion's den.

God protected Israel on their journey when He parted the Red Sea, but destroyed Pharaoh and his army. Exodus 14.

I love the story about Peter when he had been cast into jail awaiting execution for preaching the gospel. He was asleep and God sent an angel to release his chains, for him to put on his cloak, and lead him out of the jail, past the guards, through the gate, and into the street to freedom. Acts 12:3-18

God protected Paul in a vicious storm on the sea [9]
After that happened their ship ran aground and started to break up so that they had to swim to shore. The natives had built a fire on the beach to warm them. Paul gathered some sticks and as he laid them on the fire a deadly snake came out of the fire and bit his hand. God protected Paul and the Scripture states,*⁴And when the barbarians saw the venomous beast hang on his hand, they said among themselves, No doubt this man is a murderer, whom, though he hath escaped the sea, yet vengeance suffereth not to live. ⁵And he shook off the beast into the fire, and felt no harm. ⁶Howbeit they looked when he should have swollen, or fallen down dead suddenly: but after they had looked a great while, and saw no harm come to him, they changed their minds, and said that he was a god.* Acts 28:4-6

God also uses animals and other creatures to protect. God enabled a donkey to speak so that Balaam would not be slain. He used a large fish to protect His servant Jonah from drowning.

I read of two missionaries in Malaya who had an experience with God's special protection.

They were returning home from a trip they had taken with money they had received from a bank for their hospital. It was a long journey and it was turning dark so they decided to sleep on a hill by the road until it became light again. They made it home the next day.

A few weeks went by and one of the missionaries went to the states for furlough. He attended a prayer meeting and told what happened that night beside the road.

He told told them after they got back home a few weeks later a native of the area came to their hospital. He said he recognized one of the missionaries.

The native, who was a bandit, went on and told the missionaries he and 16 others were going to rob them of the money they had seen them get from the bank while they were sleeping on the hill, but there were 16 soldiers with swords circled around the missionaries and they didn't want to fight them.

God had sent His angels to protect the missionaries.

; One Sunday evening when I was pastor on the Oregon Coast, a member of our congregation told of a miraculous experience she had had that week. She told us she was travelling on highway 38 and rounding a curve she was faced by two trucks side by side coming straight at her. She knew she was a goner. But the next thing she knew she looked in her rear-view mirror and saw their tail lights. Highway 38 was a narrow two-lane highway at that time and there was no room for her car to go between the two trucks. The only explanation we came to was God had delivered and protected her that night.

But you say, "**What about the times it seems God doesn't protect us and save us from danger?** God protected Job from Satan, yet there came a time when He allowed Satan to take away his family, his possessions, and his health but Job's answer helps us

*⁷So went Satan forth from the presence of the LORD, and smote Job with sore boils from the sole of his foot unto his crown. ⁸And he took him a potsherd to scrape himself withal; and he sat down among the ashes. ⁹Then said his wife unto him, Dost thou still retain thine integrity? curse God, and die. ¹⁰But he said unto her, Thou speakest as one of the foolish women speaketh. What? shall we receive good at the hand of God, and shall we not receive evil? In all this did not Job sin with his lips.* Job 2:7-10

God allowed King Herod to chop off John the Baptist's head. He allowed James, the brother of John, to be killed by Herod the same time He delivered Peter from prison. He allowed Satan to attack the Apostle Paul with his messenger to cause a thorn in Paul's flesh but Paul said it kept him from being conceited and to know the grace and power of God in his life.

When Peter cut off the ear of the servant of the High Priest to protect Jesus as He was seized by a crowd sent by the chief priests and elders of the people the in the Garden of Gethsemane, He said to Peter, *"Put your sword back in its place...for all who draw the sword will die by the sword. Do you think I can not call on my Father, and he will at once put at my disposal more than twelve legions of angels? But how then would the Scriptures be fulfilled that say it must happen in this way?"* Matthew 26:52-54 Before Pilate, when He was on trial, Jesus said, *"You would have no power over me if it were not given to you from above.*

*Therefore the one who handed me over to you is guilty of a greater sin."* John 19:11

In conclusion, we need to remember God is sovereign. The Bible says, *"In his heart a man plans his course, but the LORD determines his steps."* Proverbs 16:9.

The important thing is to realize that we are in God's hands and He is in control. Sometimes He sees fit to protect us and at other times He allows things to come into our lives so that He will accomplish His plan in our lives and in the world. He knows our need just like He knows the needs of the birds of the air. Let us give thanks this Thanksgiving season for His watchful, protective care over us 24 hours a day.

# A CHEERFUL HEART
# GOD'S GIFT
### March 2006

Little Amy was visiting her grandfather's farm. Grandpa, a religious man, always serious and somber, would tolerate no merriment. Seeking relief from the oppressive gloom, little Amy wandered out to the barn where she spotted a donkey. Noting its sad look, she said dolefully as she patted its long face, "Poor donkey, you've got grandpa's religion, too." Christians need to realize that humor is an important part of a Christian's life.

Proverbs 17:22 states: "A cheerful heart is good medicine, but a crushed spirit dries up the bones." NIV In the book of Ecclesiastes Solomon wrote, "There is a time to weep and a time to laugh." (3:4)

Have you ever thought abut the fact that of all the in the world, man can laugh? Why is it that when a person hears something funny, he begins to laugh and the whole body reacts, and if it is really funny, tears come from his eyes. The Bible tells us when God created man He said, "Let us make make man in our image, in our likeness." (Gen. 1:26) Laughter is part of that image.

Abraham Lincoln said, "God must have meant us to laugh. Else He would not have made so any mules, parrots, monkeys and human beings."

Several years ago I read a book by Leslie Flynn entitled *Serve Him with Mirth."* (Zondervan Publishing House, Grand Rapids, Michigan) I cherish that book and have kept it in my library. Many of the thoughts in his book have been planted in my mind by his detailed study of humor in the Bible and what humor consists of. So any credit for this article goes to his extensive study on the subject.

The Bible is full of all kinds of humor.

There is good humor and bad humor. Needless to say humor has been misused, and today is perverted in many ways. The Apostle Paul in his day wrote to the members of the church in Ephesus, stating, "³But fornication, and all uncleanness, or covetousness, let it not be once named among you, as becometh saints; ⁴Neither filthiness, nor foolish talking, nor jesting, which are not convenient: but rather giving of thanks. ⁵For this ye know, that no whoremonger, nor unclean person, nor covetous man, ho is an idolater, hath any inheritance in the kingdom of Christ and of God. ⁶Let no man deceive you with vain words: for because of these things cometh the wrath of God upon the children of disobedience. obscenity, foolish talk or coarse joking, which are out of place, but rather thanksgiving." (Ephesians 5:3, 4)

Red Skelton, the famous comedian of yesteryear, was bothered at the end of his life by the off color and sexual comedy that had come into TV comedy. His shows were composed of clean comedy with a lot of laughs. Today one has a hard time finding programs with clean humor.

I have read in newspaper and magazine articles that laughter is an important part in the healing of a person. There have been studies done to show that patients in hospitals recovered from their illnesses faster when they were subjected to humorous visuals. What person hasn't had relief from grief over a lost loved one when they have times of remembering the funny things that happened with them when they were alive. Laughter is a wonderful emotion to experience in our lives.

Here are some places in the Bible where humor is evident.. A donkey speaks Numbers 22:29-35 Elijah taunting the prophets of Baal Kings 18:27; Peter knocking at the door Acts 12:13-16.

I want to close this article with a story I have told from the pulpit several times to illustrate using humor to illustrate a spiritual truth.

Dr. Walter Wilson told a story of a ten year old boy who wanted to be a preacher. When his black cat died one night, he thought this was an opportunity to start training for the ministry. He secured a shoebox and tenderly placed the corpse therein. Since the cat had died with its head to one angle, it could not be placed face up as he had seen in coffins at funerals, so he cut a hole in the lid of the box. This let the tail protrude so that visiting friends could see some part of the cat.

He had dug a grave in the back yard.

The sermon was given on the front porch. The procession marched to the back yard where the cat was gently lowered into the grave. When the boy filled the grave, the cat's tail protruded above the ground using the tail for a handle to examine the cat's condition. After a few such times, the tail no longer held, but broke off, leaving the body buried.

Dr. Wilson asked if this wasn't just like many troubled saints who having confessed their sins, continue to drag them up, pull them out, spread them before the Lord, weep over them afresh, forgetting God has buried them. 1 John 1:9

God has given us a gift—HUMOR.

A merry heart doeth good like a medicine
But a broken spirit drieth the bones.
Proverbs 17:22

THOUGHTS from REFLECTIONS

One thing I did when I prepared REFLECTIONS was that I always had a column with jokes in it. It was interesting that a lot of men told me that they always turned to the joke column first to read the jokes. It was like men turning to the sports page first of all in the newspaper. I have picked out some of the jokes they have enjoyed. Maybe they will give you a laugh too.

A little boy was in a relative's wedding. As he was coming down the aisle, he would take two steps, stop, and turn toward the crowd, put up his hands like claws and roar-- step, step, ROAR, all the way down the aisle. As you can imagine, the crowd was near tears from laughing so hard by the time he reached the pulpit. The little boy, however, was getting more and more distressed from all the laughing, and was also near tears by the time he reached the pulpit. When asked what he was doing, the child sniffed and said, "I was being the Ring Bear."

The Exchange

...

A man was hired to paint lines on a highway. The first day he painted 19 miles. His boss told him he would give him a raise if he kept up that pace. The next day he did only five miles and the next day after that he only painted one mile and was fired.

"It wasn't my fault," he muttered as he walked away. "I kept getting farther away from the can."

...

Norman and his wife listen to the weather report. The announcer says, "We are going to have 3 to 4 inches of snow today. You must park your car on the even numbered side of the street, so the snowplow can get through."

Norman's wife goes out and moves her car.

A week later while they are eating breakfast, the radio announcer says, "We are expecting 4 to 5 inches of snow today. You must park your car on the odd numbered side of the street, so the snowplow can get through."

Norman's wife goes out and moves her car again.

The next week they are having breakfast again, when the radio announcer says, "

"We are expecting 10 to 12 inches of snow today."

Norman's wife says, "Honey, I don't know what to do?"

Norman says, "Why don't you just leave the car in the garage this time?"

----

"Ladies and gentlemen," blared the announcer at the rodeo. Rusty Davis will now perform the dangerous breath-taking feat of galloping up to his bandanna and picking it off the ground with his teeth as he passes. Let'er go, Rusty!"

The drums rolled, the chute opened, and out came Rusty on his swift Palomino. Nearer and nearer to the handkerchief he came. Just as he reached it, Rusty swung low from the saddle. He and the horse sped past, but the red handkerchief still lay on the ground. An embarrassed silence gripped the stands.

Rusty wheeled the horse and galloped over to the announcer. There was a hasty conference. Then the announcer turned to the microphone and proclaimed. "Ladies and gentlemen, Rusty Davis will now ride back and pick up his bandanna, and his teeth."

...

A man arrived home from work and was greeted at the door by his wife. "I have good news and bad news," she told him.

"Give me the good news first," he said.

"The air bag works."

## H0W TO TELL THE WEATHER

Go to your back door and look for the dog. If the dog is at the door and he is wet, it's probably raining. But if the dog is standing there really soaking wet, it is probably raining really hard.

If the dog's fur looks like it's been rubbed the wrong way, it's probably windy.

If the dog has snow on his back, it's probably snowing.

Of course, to be able to tell the weather like this, you have to leave the dog outside all the time, especially if you expect bad weather.        Sincerely, The CAT

...

Upon entering a country store, a man noticed a little a harmless old hound dog asleep on the floor beside the cash register. noticed a sign posted on the glass door warning "Danger! Beware of dog.

"Is that the dog folks are suposed to beware of?" he asked the owner of the country store?

"Yep, , that's him," came the reply.

The stranger couldn't help but be amused. "That certainly doesn't look like a dangerous dog to me. Why in the world would you post the sign?"

"Because," the owner explained, "Before I posted that sign, people kept tripping over him."

...

After she woke up, a woman told her husband, "I just dreamed that you gave me a pearl necklace for Valentine's Day. What do you think it means?

"You'll know tonight," he said

.That evening, the man came home with a small package and gave it to his wife. Delighted, she opened it to find a book entitled "The Meaning of Dreams."

...

"Your wife used to be terribly nervous. Now she is cool and composed like a cucumber, What cured her?"

""The doctor did. He told her that her kind of nervousness was the usual system of advanced age.

## A SMILE

The thing that goes the farthest toward making life worth
   while,
That costs the least and does the most, is just a pleasant
   smile.

The smile that bubbles from the heart that loves its fellow
   men,
Will drive away the clouds of gloom and coax the sun again.

It's full of worth and goodness, too, with manly kindness sent;
It's worth a million dollars, and it doesn't cost a cent.

There is no room for sadness when we see a cheery smile;
It always has the same good look; it's never out of style;

It nerves us on to try again when failure makes us blue;
The dimples of encouragement are good for me and you.

It pays the highest interest—for it is merely lent;
It's worth a million dollars, and it doesn't cost a cent.

A smile comes very easy—you wrinkle up with cheer
A hundred times before you can squeeze out a salty tear;

It ripples out, moreover, to the heartstrings that will tug
And always leave an echo that is very like a hug,

So, smile away! Folks understand what by a smile is
   meant;
It's worth a million dollars, and it doesn't cost a cent.

# CLOSING THOUGHTS

Dear Reader,

I hope I have filled your mind with good thoughts and helped fulfill Philippians 4:8 in your life.

In these times Satan has been busy creating thoughts that defile our thinking. Our minds are like a computer and whatever we put in them are there until we die. I know there are things I wish I had not put into my mind that have come up when I didn't expect them to and wished I had never allowed them to enter.

There is a book that I recommend that helps us in our thought life. It was written by the one who created us and the book is the Bible. Read it and enjoy it.

Well, what happened after Wilma and Bob read THOUGHTS from REFLECTIONS? That will be told if they have another Bible study with the pastor if the Lord leads him to do one, and some more apple pies baked by Wilma.

# ‚ACKNOWLEDGEMENTS

Nathan & Vicki Strong10.5, A New Normal, 1367 Creek Road
IRASBURG VT 05845 (802)754-2790 victonasstrong@juno.com
Used by permission

Betty Swinford, "The Promise of God", *Pulpit Helps,* published by AMG
Publishers, Chattanooga, TN 37421

Richard Carlson, DON'T SWEAT THE SMALL STUFF and it's all small
stuff, Ph. D. (Hyperion, New York)

*CHRISTIAN CLIPPING,* 11004 COBBS FERRY COURT, NEW PORT\
RICHEY, FL 34654

Paul Hutchens, *My Life and I,* The Sugar Creek Press, Cascade,
Colorado, 1962. Used by permission

J.A.Gillmartin,Sheepcribone,blogstop.com, 'What About Bob?" , quoted
in *Pulpit Helps,* published by AMG Publishers, Chattanooga, TN 37421

Leslie B. Flynn, Serve Him With Mirth, Zondervan Publishing House,
Grand Rapids, Michigan, 1960

Joe McKeever, Cartoons by Joe McKeever, 601 Park Ridge Drive, River
Ridge, LA 70. Used by permission.

*Our Daily Bread®,,©,2014 .*by RBC Ministries, MI 49501    Reprinted by
permission. All rights reserved.

PRAIRIE OVERCOMER, , "Peril –and Prayer" , Three Hills, Alta, Prairie
Institute

*Pulpit Helps,* published by AMG Publishers, Chattanooga, TN 37421
Used by permission

"The Whale Said 'Thank You'" SAN FRANCISCO CHRONICLE, quoted
in *CHRISTIAN CLIPPINGS,* October, November, December, 2009

The Exchange, Cathedral Press, Box 419, Long Prairie, M N . 56347,
www.cathedralpress.com Used by permission

THOUGHTS from REFLECTIONS

*Vine's Complete Expository Dictionary of Old and New Testament Words,* Thomas Nelson Publishers Nashville, Camden, New York, 1985

*Word Pictures in the New Testament,* Archibald Thomas Robertson, Broadman Press, 1930..

*WUEST'S WORD STUDIES,* Kenneth S Wuest, Wm. B. Eerdmans Publishing Company, The Pastoral Epistle.

O LORD, thou hast searched me, and known *me.*
Thou knowest my downsitting and mine uprising,
Thou understandest my thought afar off.
Thou compassest my path and my lying down
and art acquainted with all my ways.
Psalm 139:1-3

41145113R00066

Made in the USA
San Bernardino, CA
05 November 2016